I'll Walk With God

I'll Walk With God

Hilda Gordon

NEW WINE PRESS

Dedication

In thanksgiving to the Lord for His guidance and direction; to my Mother and Father, who laid those early foundations and to Bob, my husband and Jonathan, my son, for their constant love and encouragement as daily we adventure together with God.

New Wine Press
PO Box 17
Chichester PO20 6YB
England

First published in 1988 by Marshall Morgan and Scott Publications Ltd.

Unless otherwise indicated, all Scripture references quoted are from the Holy Bible New International Version © 1973, 1978 New York International Bible Society, published in Great Britain by Hodder & Stoughton Ltd.

ISBN: 1 874367 19 1

Printed in England by Clays Ltd, St Ives plc.

Contents

Acknowledgements

This book was written in the centre of a very busy household, therefore there are a number of people to whom I owe many thanks. Words are totally inadequate to express my gratitude to my dear friend Jo McCulloch, who has been my constant support and adviser, and without whose help in getting the manuscript onto computer and then checked, this book would not have been written. To Pat Nightingale, who from time to time, very willingly stepped in and took over the running of the household. Also to Peter Goddard, who so ably designed the cover, and to the household here for their love and understanding as from time to time I have opted out of the home scene.

Romans 8:28

'And we know that all things work together for good to them that love God to them that are the called according to His purpose.' (AV)

Oswald Chambers

'It is well to remember that it is the 'together' of circumstances that works for good. God changes our circumstances; sometimes they are bright, sometimes they are the opposite; but God makes them work together for our good.'

Chapter 1

By Way of Introduction

Prayer is an exciting adventure with God! That may seem a wild statement. It certainly would have been to me until 1974, when God came into my life in the power of His Holy Spirit and filled my dry, barren heart with His very presence.

Through the pages of this book I want to share with you the experiences through which God has taken me in His divine purpose and show you that real prayer can be, and is, an exciting adventure with the living God.

I was born in Dublin in 1941. My parents were regular members of the Church of Ireland, where I attended Sunday School. On Sunday morning I would go along to the Church of Ireland Sunday School and then in the afternoon I was taken along to the Open Brethren Sunday School. Looking back, I really praise God for faithful Sunday School teachers, who gave me verses of Scripture to learn and passages of Scripture to recite. Little did I know then how valuable an exercise that was. It was where the seed was first sown and the love for the Scriptures first started. Many years were to elapse before I would realise the full significance and importance of those early foundations.

When I was ten years old my parents moved to England to the city of Lincoln. Having scoured the city's churches we finally made our spiritual home in the Open Brethren Assembly. Again I thank God for the men who loved the Word of God and passed that on to me. Alf Garnet, my old Bible class teacher, really made the Bible stories live. He had a model of the Ark of the Covenant and explained to us in fine detail every little significant component. The excitement we had tracing Paul's missionary journeys and the fun of gathering round the piano and singing gospel hymns. All of this like a legacy was poured into my lap and I can see now how privileged I was to have been born into a Christian home and brought up in such warm fellowship.

I became a Christian in my early teens, through the ministry of Billy Graham in this country. It was his simplicity and directness in handling the Word of God that impressed me. I cannot remember the exact message on that night when I became a Christian, but this I do remember – I became very aware of my need of Jesus. What he had done at Calvary on my behalf demanded a response from my heart. I can still remember the excitement and joy I experienced that evening as I skipped home to relate all that happened to my family.

The fellowship, to which I belonged, were thrilled and pointed out to me right from the start the necessity of reading the Scriptures each day and also daily prayer; then I would grow spiritually. Finding a system of daily Bible readings was not a real problem, there was quite a number from which to choose, but prayer was quite a different matter. How did I tackle this one? At first there was no real problem. In the excitement and innocence of my new found faith in Jesus I would just naturally reach out to God my Father for my needs, and praise and worship were almost automatic. How quickly we lose that original trust and simplicity; just like a baby growing up. At first that complete dependence and confidence in Dad and Mum, but before long he begins to assert his own independence and question the authority and wider experience of the parents. So it is with us as Christians. Questions begin to flood our minds as God begins to present us with bigger challenges and larger steps of faith are called for. Is He really that mighty God? Can He really enable me to remove mountains? Can He perform miracles in my life and experience or is that just for Bible characters and special men and women of faith?

At this particular stage in my walk with God I would have loved to have known someone like 'Fletcher of Madeley'. He was a fellow worker with Wesley and a great teacher of the eighteenth century, who used to lecture theological students. After the lecture, whatever the topic may have been – the Word of God, the fullness of the Holy Spirit or prayer, he would close the lecture and say, 'That is the theory. Now will those who want the practice come along up to my room?' Again and again they closed their books and went away to his room where the hour's theory would be followed by one or two hours prayer. However there wasn't a 'Fletcher of Madeley' about when I became a Christian, but a year or so later the Lord taught me, through an incident in my own life, that he was a mighty God and He could perform miracles, even in my life. It wasn't just for special people or Bible characters. I'll come back to this later.

I chose Romans 8:28 as the title verse for this first chapter because it exactly sums up for me God's purposes in all the ins and outs and ups and downs that go to make up what we call life. 'We know that in all things God works for the good of those who love him'. There was a time when I thought that God was just at work in the good things that happened to me, but looking back over my life I can trace the hand of God in 'all' things', whether we describe them as good, bad, hard, tough or dark, God allows them and will use them to discipline, correct, upbuild and take us on to maturity in Christ. Today we may be enjoying the green pastures and revival, tomorrow it may be a dark valley experience but God is at work in both for our good. He can bring victory out of the most disastrous appearing circumstances if we are willing to trust Him. God's prime purposes for us is to build the character of Christ in us; far more important than service or ministry is what we *are*, not what we do. Everything that happens to us in life should draw us into closer communion with the Lord. God is wanting to change us 'from one degree of glory to another' (2 Cor. 3:18), (RSV), until we are transformed into the likeness of His

11

Son. This happens in the 'secret place' as we fellowship with the Father and take time to listen as well as talk. God has a plan for each one of us and this is where He reveals it – step by step, stage by stage.

I once heard a fascinating story of how two women who were studying the Scriptures came across a verse which says, 'For He will be like a refiner's fire or a launderer's soap. He will sit as a refiner and purifier of silver' (Mal. 3:3). They pondered over the verse and decided they would understand the significance and meaning of it far better if they knew how silver was refined and purified. So they took a trip to the local silversmiths to ask the question.

He was very helpful and happy to explain the process to them. A furnace needed to be heated to a very hot heat. The silver was then placed in the furnace. Once the silver had been placed in the furnace the smith's eyes never left it until the process was complete. This explanation really helped the ladies in their understanding and they thanked him for his trouble. They were about to leave when he said, 'Just one more thing I forgot to tell you. I know the process is complete when I can see my reflection in the silver.'

What an illustration of how the Lord works in our lives. He knows exactly what we are going through,

> 'For we do not have a high priest who is unable to sympathise with our weaknesses, but we have one who has been tempted in every way, just as we are – yet was without sin.' (Heb. 4:15).

When the heat is on His all-seeing eyes never leave us for a minute. We begin to yell at the first twinge of pressure, but He knows how much we can bear, He tells us so in His word,

> 'No temptation has seized you except what is common to man. And God is faithful, He will not let you be tempted beyond what you can bear. But when you are tempted, He will also provide a way out so that you can stand up under it' (1 Cor. 10:13).

The Father is an extremely good judge. He is sovereign and knows best, because He can see the end from the beginning. Like a professional archer He pulls back the bow, tight as can be, aims the arrow at the target and when both are exactly in position He fires and hits the bullseye. God's purpose in all this is to see more of the life and character of Jesus demonstrated in us.

'The crucible for silver and the furnace for gold but the Lord tests the heart.' (Prov. 17:3).

'Lord teach us to pray.'
Luke 11:1

'Abide in me'
John 15:4

Andrew Murray

'Let us resolve at once that it will be the one characteristic of our life and worship, to continually, humbly, and truthfully wait on God. We may rest assured that the One who made us for Himself that He might give Himself to us and in us, will never disappoint us. In waiting on Him we will find rest and joy and strength and the supply of every need.

My soul, wait only on God!'

D. M. McIntyre

'While we abide in Christ we ought not to allow ourselves to be discouraged by the apparent slowness of our advancement in grace. In nature growth proceeds with varying speed. Sibbes compares the progressive sanctification of believers to the increase in the "herbs and trees," which "grow at the root in winter, in the leaf in summer, and in the seed in autumn." The first of these forms of increase seems very slow; the second is more rapid; the third rushes on to full maturity – in a few days of early autumn a field of grain will seem to ripen more than in weeks in midsummer.

Communion with God discovers the excellence of His character, and by beholding Him the soul is transformed. Holiness is conformity to Christ, and this is secured by a growing intimacy with Him.'

Chapter 2

An Intimate Relationship

In my late teens I struggled with prayer. It was very much a hit and miss situation. There were times when I really felt I had touched the throne of God, but for most of the time there seemed to be something sadly missing. Looking back I now realise how long I lived with a wrong idea of what prayer was all about. I had somehow got it into my head that prayer was something I did for God for 15–30 minutes each day and it seemed to be completely unrelated to anything else that went on in my life. Another thing had crept in. I had begun to ask God for things that were only humanly possible, so He wouldn't be overtaxed and I wouldn't be disappointed. The Lord had so much to teach me about real communion with Him. From those early days of trust and eager expectation, I had now brought God down to my level and reduced him to a size I could easily manage.

As is so often the case, when we are stuck we look around at other people What their performance is like; how they tackle, in this case, prayer. I began to scan the fellowship and take note of the people who in my estimation, knew how to pray. Then I would pay particular attention to all I observed and copy them. Needless to say, copying other people was not the answer; even though I had all the jargon and terminology off to a tee, it was still empty and powerless.

This was a very barren period. The further I went along the more dried up and empty I became. Prayer became meaningless and the Scriptures just words, although I

15

would not admit this to anyone or even to myself. I held out like this for quite sometime and was determined not to give in until I had to.

By this time I was married to Bob and we had adopted our son Jonathan, who was just six months and very active. We were living in Durham, where Bob was a URC minister and also chaplain to St Mary's College in the University. Life was pretty full and very hectic. It was our first call in ministry and we were anxious that everything went well, people were cared for and the church ran smoothly. All was well and under control until there began to be some strange rumours and rumblings in Durham about the Baptism in the Holy Spirit. We ignored these reports at first, but then things began to get serious and one church after another appeared to be affected. It was most disconcerting. What on earth was happening?

Bob then received an invitation to a Charismatic Ministers Conference up in Edinburgh, led by the Fountain Trust. I didn't like the sound of it at all and was really very fearful at the thought of Bob going to anything of that nature. My worst fears were confirmed when Bob rang me half way through the week and announced that he wasn't quite sure what was going on but it was pretty powerful. It sent a cold shiver down my spine. At the end of the week Bob arrived home singing strange songs and grinning all over his face. There was no doubt about it, he was different. Full of joy and life and he tried desperately to convey to me just what had happened to him; but I was really not interested and hoped and prayed that one morning I would wake up and it would all be back to normal. No such luck!! In fact Bob seemed to go on in leaps and bounds, there was no holding him. My thoughts were not exactly godly. I was convinced that if ever I got my hands on the two men who laid hands on him I would strangle them. My life was busy enough. Running a manse and all that entails; endless meetings and looking after our baby son. I could really do without these disruptive experiences.

16

This state of affairs went on for three or four months, until I began to see that Bob and I were travelling on different roads. It really scared me and I could see our marriage in jeopardy.

It's amazing how the Lord uses circumstances to bring us to the end of ourselves and to desperation point. I remember one day feeling so wretched and confused, I fed Jonathan, popped him in his pram, prayed that the Lord would care for him and keep him asleep until I had sorted out, once and for all, this question of the Holy Spirit.

I went to the bedroom, got my Bible out, dropped to my knees and began reading the New Testament, starting in Acts; after all this was where it all began. I read and thumbed through Acts, Romans, 1 and 2 Corinthians and Galatians. Nothing seemed to be speaking to me and time was marching on. I cried out to the Lord to do something with my life – to touch it afresh; and so I read on until I came to Ephesians 3:16, Paul's prayer for the Ephesians, 'I pray that out of His glorious riches He may strengthen you with His power through His Spirit in your inner being.' Those words hit me forcefully. That was exactly what I needed. The power of His Spirit in my inner being because I was dead and empty. I jumped up, thanked the Lord and ran downstairs to get the supper. I didn't experience any of those great feelings of joy and elation, nor did I speak in tongues, like I had read in books, but for the first time in years God's Word had penetrated into my being and I had felt His touch.

Bob came in after a busy day and we sat down together for supper. He began with his usual question of how had the day gone? He wasn't quite prepared for my reaction as I burst into tears and began to blurt out all that had happened during the afternoon. After several hours talking and sharing, I realised that we were now both walking the same road again and communicating with one another in a way we had not done for months. The next mornings as we opened the Scriptures together and prayed, the joy came flooding in. The Word of God was alive and fresh once more and I knew I was in touch with heaven. I had found that missing element. I no longer had to struggle on in my own strength, I had the Holy Spirit of God to strengthen and enable me. The God I had encountered was a 'big God' and a mighty God. Praise His Name!!

Is your deep-down heart's desire for God? His word tells us that God is very concerned with the state of your heart (1 Sam. 16:7). Even though you don't always have the time you would like, is there a longing in your heart for fellowship with the Father? Can you say this with the Psalmist? 'As the deer pants for streams of water, so my soul pants for you, O God. My soul thirsts for God, for the living God' (Ps. 42:1–2).

If your answer to this question is yes. Praise God! He can build on this as you make time for Him. Later on in this book I am going to deal with 'The Practice of Prayer'. How we go about it with the time we have at our disposal; taking into account differing groups of people.

Perhaps you find yourself in a state of apathy. Then shake yourself. This is no time to feel like this and it is also a very dangerous state in which to be. Remember what God had to say to the church at Laodicea.

'I know your deeds, that you are neither cold nor hot. I wish you were either one or the other! So, because you are lukewarm – neither hot nor cold – I am about to spit you out of my mouth. You say, "I am rich; I have acquired wealth and do not need a thing." But you do not realise that you are wretched, pitiful, poor, blind and naked. I counsel you to buy from me gold refined in the fire, so that you can become rich; and white clothes to wear, so that you can cover your shameful nakedness; and salve to put on your eyes, so that you can see.

Those whom I love I rebuke and discipline, so be earnest and repent. Here I am! I stand at the door and knock. If anyone hears my voice and opens the door, I will come in and eat with him, and he with me.

To him who overcomes, I will give the right to sit with

me on my throne, just as I overcame and sat down with my Father on His throne. He who has an ear, let him hear what the Spirit says to the churches' (Rev. 3:15–22).

We are living in urgent and exciting times. I believe we are going to see a mighty movement of God's Holy Spirit in this land of ours before too long. Don't be caught napping. Tell the Lord how you feel then invite Him to wake you from your indifference and replace it with the joy and enthusiasm you once knew. Don't be too surprised how He goes about it. He moves in mysterious ways yet His ways of working are usually very down to earth and involve everyday situations; so keep your eyes and spirit open to perceive God's movements.

Maybe you have never been baptised in the Holy Spirit. You feel the lack of power within. You are trying to do God's work in your own strength. Again the Lord invites us to

'Ask and it will be given to you; seek and you will find; knock and the door will be opened to you. For everyone who asks receives; he who seeks finds; and to him who knocks, the door will be opened.

Which of you fathers, if your son asks for a fish, will give him a snake instead? Or if he asks for an egg, will give him a scorpion? If you then, though you are evil, know how to give good gifts to your children, how much more will your Father in heaven give the Holy Spirit to those who ask Him!' (Luke 11:9–13).

If you feel like I described earlier – dry, empty and cut off from the Almighty and you long to get back to the relationship you first knew, then cry out to God.

' "You will seek me and find me when you seek me with all your heart. I will be found by you", declares the Lord.' (Jer. 29:13).

God can meet you right where you are. On the other hand you may like some help from your pastor or a mature christian friend. Very often it helps to share your difficulties with someone, so they in turn can pray with you and for you. Don't put it off any longer; and don't allow fear or pride to stand in your way. Remember the story of the prodigal son? The Father's arms are wide open and His heart towards you when you return in true repentance. As we confess to Him and receive His forgiveness so He has the robe, the ring and the sandals ready for you to put on.

> 'Now if we are children, then we are heirs – heirs of God and co-heirs with Christ, if indeed we share in His sufferings in order that we may share in His glory.' (Rom. 8:17).

Back in the family at last!!

After this encounter with the living God reading the Scriptures and prayer became a joy for me again and life took on a very different hue. I was eager to maintain and pursue my new found fellowship with the Lord. Where did I begin? Slowly it dawned on me that it was not right or necessary for me to have my own ideas on prayer, or to look at other people and read about their experiences, good as they are in their place. God had gone to the trouble of laying down principles in His Word which held good not only for Moses, Elijah, David, Isaiah, Paul and all the saints down the centuries, but for me, if I could be bothered to seek them out. After all He was the changeless one, 'the same yesterday, today and for ever.' He had not concocted or invented a new way for twentieth-century man.

When I started to search the Scriptures and look at men and women of prayer in the Bible, the Holy Spirit directed me particularly to Jesus' teaching on prayer in Luke 11. I read through the first 13 verses and asked the Lord to teach me from His Word how to pray and commune with Him.

Looking at verse 1 again of Luke 11, my eyes were drawn to the request the disciples made to Jesus. 'Lord teach us to pray.' I thought about it again and felt it was rather a strange request coming from men who had spent their days with Jesus. Surely they must have known how to pray?

The Holy Spirit began to speak to me and say, 'But you thought you knew how to pray!' Like the disciples I needed to learn. 'One day Jesus was praying in a certain place. When He finished, one of His disciples said to Him, "Lord teach us to pray."' (Luke 11:1). The disciples had just witnessed Jesus in deep communion with His Father. This was something quite different and far more dynamic from anything they had experienced in the realm of prayer. They desperately wanted to know how to have this intimate relationship with the Father which they had seen Jesus enjoying.

The Spirit took my mind through the gospels and recalled to my mind words like these: 'Jesus stayed behind a little while'; 'Jesus went on a little further'; 'Jesus went up a mountain side'; 'Jesus stayed up all night'; 'Jesus rose early in the morning'. I began to understand how often Jesus was alone with His Father. His whole concentration and heart were involved in that meeting. Nothing and no-one was allowed to intrude.

This is the first and most essential principle of real prayer, an intimate relationship with the Father through Jesus Christ. That's where we start. Find a room, a place and a time when you are not going to be disturbed. Take the Scriptures with you and open your life daily to the living God. Worship Him from your heart, praise Him for who He is, find forgiveness for your sin, a fresh anointing of His Holy Spirit and wisdom and direction for the day. Everything in each day and in your life hinges on your relationship with the Father. It was the key to the life and ministry of Jesus, while He was here on this earth. He came not to do His will, but that of His Father (John 6:38).

Jesus was in continual touch with His Father; that was the secret of His power and authority; and because He was in line with His Father's will and in a constant relationship, so as He reached out to heal, to bless, to calm the storm, to raise the dead, the Father honoured the Son. We got some insight into the depth of this relationship when we look at John 17 and see Jesus in communion with His Father, interceding for the disciples and also for all who would believe through their

21

message. His great longing was 'Father just as you are in me and I am in you. May they also be in us' (John 17.21).

This is such an important principle of prayer that you need to question yourself to see if it is active in your life. How is your relationship with the Lord? Read the first 13 verses of Luke 11 and also John 17 and ask yourself afresh, How deep is my communion with the Lord? Have I progressed over the last year, six months, three months, last week? God is always throwing out the challenge – 'Put me to the test . . .' We were made for communion with God. It was sin that got in the way and stopped that; but Jesus has made that way back to the Father and He longs to be involved in all of our living. There is not one area of our lives in which He is not interested.

How much about the character of God do you know? Of course we can hear about this from friends or a sermon, or from a book. We can even read about the attributes of God's character from the Bible, but do you know them to be real for you? For instance, can you say I know God is a God of faithfulness because He did such and such a thing in my life and experience? Or do you just live on hearsay? There is no need to. The Father longs to demonstrate to you personally that He is a faithful God, a God of love, of provision, of patience, a God of might and miracle, who is 'able to do far more abundantly above all we ask or even imagine' (Eph. 3:20).

Why not start today on a road to discovery?

I find it almost impossible to put down on paper, or relate in a book all that is going on inside of me, but I pray that you will glean from these pages what is in my spirit; that my longing and pursuit of God will be like a contagious disease and picked up by your spirit.

Let me encourage you to do this. Always stretch out for more than you think you can handle. That may seem a strange thing to say, but I bless the men and women of God who dropped me in at the 'deep end', because it made me swim and long for more! I didn't understand everything in fine detail, that didn't matter. There was always one thing that really hit me and the Lord would 'home-in' on that. It's not always the big spiritual issues that God wants to underline but quite often small things. For instance, I remember the day the Lord asked me to kneel to pray. You see the Lord knows us so personally and knows exactly the next step each one of us needs in our ongoing relationship with Him. In your case it may be something quite different. Whatever it is, be sure to be obedient, otherwise you will hold up your progress. The Lord won't move on to the next lesson until we have heard Him clearly and put into action what He is saying to us right now.

'He who is faithful in a very little is fathful also in much' (Luke 16:10), (RSV).

If we really examine ourselves we are lazy at heart. Very happy to be spoon-fed, rest back on our laurels and live on either yesterday's blessing or someone else's experience. Stretch out and know God for yourself. Don't rush and don't be impatient! There is an art in building a good relationship, just as there is in learning to play a musical instrument. It doesn't happen overnight. First come the scales and they seem to go on endlessly. How we long to get on to the real music – symphonies and concertos; but we haven't gone far along the road before we understand how necessary and foundational the scales are. If we haven't learnt them thoroughly we are in real trouble when we come to the more difficult pieces.

'Let us know, let us press on to know the Lord; His going forth is sure as the dawn; He will come to us as the showers, as the spring rains that water the earth' (Hos. 6:3).

There is always room for improvement when it comes to our relationship with the Lord. When I have written this book and shared with you all that the Lord has taught me of Himself and done in my life so far, it will be out of date, or at least it should be. God is continually taking us into new areas and greater

23

depths of Himself, as we fellowship with Him. The apostle Paul, who walked closely with the Lord, after a lifetime of ministry, was still able to say

'All I want is to know Christ and to experience the power of His resurrection, to share in His sufferings and become like Him in His death, in the hope that I myself will be raised from death to life' (Phil. 3:10–11, Good News Bible).

When it comes to prayer we are always in a school. The more we get to know Jesus, so the more we realise there is to know. There are heights to climb and depths to explore we have never as yet comprehended.

'Oh, the depth of the riches of the wisdom and knowledge of God!
How unsearchable His judgements, and His paths beyond tracing out!
For from Him and through Him and to Him are all things. To Him be the glory for ever! Amen.' (Rom. 11:33, 36).

We begin this personal relationship when we are born again into the family of God; but this is just the introduction and like any human relationship if it is not nurtured and developed it will die.

We know only too well what it is like when we are introduced to someone whose company we really enjoy. We promise to keep in touch with them and then, through one thing and another, fail to do so. A sadness grips us. We realise we have let them down and lost out on what could have been the more embarrassing it is to contact them again and even worse if we happen to bump into them in the street. We don't quite know what to say and we can't look them straight in the eye. Then we need to make our apologies and begin again. If we do this too often the person gets rather disillusioned with our unreliability and gives up on us. Humanly speaking, we get our just desserts. Yet how often is this just how we treat the Lord? No wonder we make so little progress, when we are such fickle people.

Praise God, He does not treat us according to our sins and failures but is plenteous in mercy and abounding in grace. Nevertheless this is not a let-out clause! Of course we can come back, find forgiveness and begin again, but if we really want to grow spiritually, let us be disciplined and determined in our spirits, with the Lord's help, to keep our appointments with God. Strive to be those people in whom God can trust and then our lives will begin to be fruitful towards God and man.

The Christian life is based on obedience and not on feelings. So often we do things only if we feel like it or we are in the right mood. When it comes to prayer that is most definitely the case. Our wills need to be set towards God at the beginning of each day, then as we step out in faith so He pours in the strength, the power and the victory.

There are days when we get up in the morning feeling out of sorts or with a fit of the 'blues', when everything in us wants to run away from God, rather than be in His presence. We tell ourselves we can't possibly meet with the Lord in the condition we are in. I've done this endless times, until one day I realised it was a ploy of Satan to keep me away from fellowship with the Lord and consequently out of relationship.

Look at the Psalmist; he comes to God in every conceivable mood. When he is on top of the world and his heart is full of praise and worship. When he is down in the dumps and in a state of self-pity. When he is having a hard time from his enemies and they are on his tail and threatening him. Also in those dark times when he is alone and unsure and wonders where God is. The great thing about the Psalmist is that he knew that in whatever state or mood he was in he needed to meet with his God, tell Him about it and find the refreshment and answer that he knew no-one else could give him.

'O Lord, you have searched me and you know me.
You know when I sit and when I rise; you perceive my
thoughts from afar.

You discern my going out and my lying down;
you are familiar with all my ways' (Ps. 139:1–3).

Why try to run away? No-one understands like Jesus.

We have an old record of W. E. Sangster. He was a great
Methodist preacher. On the record he tells of how John
Wesley, that great man of God, used to go through very
dark depressions from time to time. They were so bad, he
wondered where God was and yet this man in obedience
was up at five o'clock each morning to pray, regardless of
feelings, knowing that his God would eventually pierce
through the thick darkness with His shaft of divine light.

There is a saying that 'the good is the enemy of the best!'
If we are to go deep in our relationship with the Lord then
we need to be disciplined and orderly, especially with our
time. We need to know when to say no. The hour in the
afternoon or evening that we promised to set aside for
reading the Scriptures or prayer. What happened to it? So
many other things and people come in and demand that
time. Satan always sees to it that they are all very good,
legitimate causes and you are really not being very fair to all
parties concerned, unless you give in. I used to fall for this
one every time, until one day I decided to stick to my
promise and give God the time and priority. I was amazed
how everything fell into place, nobody suffered and I was
certainly much the richer.

How I wish I had been quicker to learn in the beginning
and not wasted so much time blowing hot and cold and
going up and down like a yo-yo. I haven't reached
perfection yet, but with Paul I can say,

'Forgetting what is behind and straining towards what is
ahead. I press on towards the goal . . .' (Phil. 3:13–14).

Let me, at this juncture encourage you, especially if you
have recently become a Christian, to cultivate a desire for
the Word of God and keep regular communion with the

Lord. He longs for fellowship with you. Get to know Him: His character, His ways of working, His unfailing love and the great plans and purposes He had for you. He is a God of infinite patience to those whose hearts are set toward Him.

Abide in Me

Before we leave this all-important subject of our relationship with the Lord let's look at John 15. Read the first seventeen verses and ask the Lord to give you a new appreciation of their meaning. We can get so familiar with Scripture, especially well known passages, that it just goes over our heads, without hitting us where it needs to and taking root.

This is perhaps the most illustrative chapter in the whole Bible when it comes to giving us a clear picture of what our relationship is to the Father through Jesus. Jesus said 'I am the true vine and my Father is the gardener . . . you are the branches.'

It is an amazing concept that as we come into the Kingdom of God through Jesus, so we are grafted into the 'true vine' and we become partakers of the very nature of the Son of God. Allow this thought to sink into your spirit, because the repercussions are mind-blowing. Everything that Jesus is in nature and character potentially is yours, because you are a branch of that vine. Therefore the more you feed from the divine sap, so the stronger you grow; leaves begin to appear and then the fruit.

The word 'remain' or 'abide' occurs no less than eleven times in this short passage. Jesus was trying to get a very important message across to the disciples. He was saying that just as He was at one with the Father, part of all the Father represented, and the fruit was there for all to see, so, as we remain in Jesus, in His love, and allow His word to cleanse and shape us, a fruitful life will be the outcome.

'We are members of His body,
We are objects of His love,
We're partakers of His holiness,
We are citizens of heaven above.

We're partakers of His suffering,
We're partakers of His grace,
We shall be changed to be like Him,
When we see Him face to face.'

In John 14 Jesus goes into some detail to explain to the disciples the Father/Son relationship.

'Don't you believe that I am in the Father, and that the Father is in me? The words I say to you are not just my own. Rather, it is the Father, living in me, who is doing His work. Believe me when I say that I am in the Father and the Father is in me; or at least believe on the evidence of the miracles themselves. I tell you the truth, anyone who has faith in me will do what I have been doing. He will do even greater things than these, because I am going to the Father.' (John 14:10–12).

In verse 12 you will notice that Jesus is saying everything that the Father and Son enjoy in fellowship and communion terms, is yours as you abide in the Son. The result of that union in the life of Jesus was fruitfulness, – that is the will and purposes and desires of the Father were fulfilled, so as we abide in the vine we will see the Father's plans and desires for our lives and His kingdom accomplished.

'Every branch that bears fruit He prunes, so that it will be even more fruitful' – Don't try and dodge the pruning knife! The Lord does this for a purpose. When we have had a fruitful time the big temptation is to live on that experience indefinitely; but the Father knows it is necessary to trim us right back in order that the next season's fruit is even bigger and better. I know very little about gardening, but I remember watching a friend of mine, who was a very experienced gardener, pruning roses. I almost had to shut my eyes as I watched her cutting a bush right back almost to a stump. A bush that produced such lovely fragrant blooms, reduced to nothing. But she knew exactly what she was

28

doing, because the bush began to feed afresh from the root and grow healthy branches and produce even more beautiful roses.

You see the fruit we produce is for picking and eating not just for decoration. Therefore when people have eaten that fruit and the branch is stripped bare, the Father comes along with His pruning-knife and lops it off. That in turn drives us back to the vine for more nourishment in order to grow more fruit. The life is in the vine and it's the vine that produces the good fruit.

'Apart from me you can do nothing' – I well remember an occasion not long after Bob and I had been filled with the Spirit when we led a student retreat up to the shores of Loch Etive in Scotland. We were coming towards the end of a terrific week of fellowship and learning together, when on the Thursday evening, during the meeting the Holy Spirit fell with power and each student in turn received the fullness of the Spirit. Bob and I were used along with a friend of ours, Malcolm Hanson, to minister to those students. It was a great night of rejoicing but in the morning I felt dreadful. I couldn't even bring myself to get out of bed. I felt so empty as if I had given everything I ever knew or believed away. There seemed to be nothing left inside for me. Of course that was exactly what had happened. All the fruit of the last few months had been picked. Malcolm Hanson came up to the bedroom and ministered to me and very rightly pointed out that I needed to go back to the source of living water and receive again from the fountain of life.

I learnt a very important lesson that day, which I have never forgotten, 'Go on being filled with the Spirit' (Eph. 5:18). It is not just a once for all experience, but a daily necessity.

'If a man remains in me and I in him he will bear much fruit.' – Trees are used on a number of occasions in the Scriptures to illustrate a spiritual principle. Turn to Jeremiah 17 and read verses 5 to 8. This is a passage of contrast. On the one hand you have verse 5,

> 'Cursed is the one who trusts in man,
> who depends on flesh for his strength.'

and on the other hand you have verse 7,

> 'But blessed is the man who trusts in the Lord,
> whose confidence is in Him.'

It's no good relying on your own strength or putting your confidence in other people to produce fruit, not fruit that is wholesome and edifying. It is possible to produce a substitute fruit that on the outside looks all right, but inside it is bitter and tasteless. People know whether you have been with Jesus as soon as they begin to eat the fruit, whether the word you speak into their life comes just from you and your well meaning heart, or whether it is straight from the throne of God.

Verses 5 and 6 hold some pretty strong words. Take note!

> 'But blessed is the man who trusts in the Lord,
> whose confidence is in Him.
> He will be like a tree planted by the water
> that sends out its roots by the stream.
> It does not fear when the heat comes,
> its leaves are always green.
> It has no worries in the year of drought
> and never fails to bear fruit.'

How deep are your roots? Do you fear when the heat comes and the pressure is on? Are your leaves always green? Have you any worries in the year of drought? These are very valid questions to address to ourselves concerning the depth and quality of our relationship with the Lord.

A friend of mine, Angie Hindmarsh, told me of an incident which she has never forgotten. She was brought up in a south Lincolnshire village. Her father worked in the village and during the course of his work unearthed a very old brick well, which he took Angie to see. It was very interesting to see, but even more amazing was the fact that at the bottom of the well lay the roots of a tree, which when traced turned out to be the tree in the farthest corner of the field. The discovery of those very healthy roots accounted for the fact that the tree, during the drought of 1976, continued to be green and fruitful, when all the other trees looked withered and dried-up. Those roots spread out and went deep, even forcing their way through the brick, until they found a source of life, which no other tree had tapped. It was there for the other trees, they just hadn't gone deep enough.

Don't be content with a surface and shallow relationship with the Lord. Allow your roots to go deep until like the river in Ezekiel 47, you are in over the head and need to swim.

'You are the vine, we are the branches,
Keep us abiding in you,

And we'll go in your name
And we'll go in your love
That the world will surely know
That you have power to heal and to save,

You are the vine, we are the branches
Keep us abiding in you.'

Genesis 32:26

'Then he said, "Let me go for the day is breaking." But Jacob said, "I will not let you go unless you bless me."' (AV)

E. M. Bounds

'Too often we get fainthearted and quit praying at the point where we ought to begin. We let go at the very point where we should hold on strongest. Our prayers are weak because they are not impassioned by an unfailing and resistless will.'

Chapter 3

A Cry from the Heart

We see how important and fundamental a right relationship with the Lord is when we look at verse 5 of Luke 11. Here Jesus tells a story to the disciples in order to teach them some more principles of real prayer. You will see, only too clearly, why a deep, living relationship with the Father is basic and implicit in this story. Jesus said,

> 'Suppose one of you has a friend, and he goes to him at midnight and says, "Friend, lend me three loaves of bread, because a friend of mine on a journey has come to me, and I have nothing to set before him."'

What a predicament to be in! Empty! Not a thing in the pantry. Notice these situations always happen at the worst possible moment. Midnight! The shops are shut and everyone is in bed. What is he going to do? Then he remembers his friend. Now there is no way he would go and hammer on his friend's door at midnight, knowing that he and his family were already in bed, without having a very well established heart knowledge of the man. He knows he is someone on whom he can depend in his hour of need, so he asks and asks and continues to bang on the door until he gets his request met.

God allows situations like this to happen in our experience to show us that our trust needs to be wholly and fully in Him. We haven't the answer ourselves and the circumstances are such that nobody else can help, so we cry out to God from our hearts. We really mean business with

Him. He is the only one who has the answer to our plight. Suddenly we realise we are praying as we have never prayed before, or at least, not for a very long time.

All the words in Scripture connected with prayer are strong words and are in one way or another linked to action. Prayer is not something you do sitting in a rocking-chair lulling yourself to sleep. No, it is very much a word associated with battle and warfare, hence the title verse of this chapter, Genesis 32:26, where Jacob wrestles with the man of God. 'Then the man said, "Let me go for it is daybreak." But Jacob replied, "I will not let you go unless you bless me."'

E. M. Bounds is so right when he says,

'Too often we get fainthearted and quit praying at the point where we ought to begin. We let go at the very point where we should hold on strongest. Our prayers are weak because they are not impassioned by an unfailing and resistless will.'

His Word says 'You will seek me and find me when you seek me with all your heart' (Jer. 29:13). Our communion with God has got to be wholehearted and single-eyed. God demands our spirit, soul and body when we fellowship with Him.

Oh for men and women of prayer today like John Hyde of India, who used to pray, 'Give me souls or I die', or John Knox, who prayed, 'Give me Scotland or I die'. They really meant it. They were not just words that fell from their lips, but a burden that weighed heavily upon their hearts and they wrestled with God for the people they loved and would not let go until the blessing came.

'Then the man said, "Your name will no longer be Jacob, but Israel, because you have struggled with God and with men and have overcome"' (Gen. 32:28).

We have been called to be co-workers with God through

prayer. To bring heaven's blessings down to this sad earth. It took the man in the story to *ask* and his friend to provide in order that the midnight caller's need be met. So it is with us and God; we need *to ask* in order for God *to provide*. This may seem a very basic thing to say but it is something we so easily forget. Be specific, let God know in particular what it is you are asking of Him. Let it come from the heart. If the man in the story couldn't be bothered to hammer on his friend's door and ask for bread, the midnight caller would have left very hungry. He might have been able to muscle up a few crumbs and maybe even a drink of water, but that would have been a very partial blessing. How often we seem so content to put up with what we can do in our own strength, instead of taking up the challenge of Malachi 3:10, ' "Put me to the test" says the Lord of hosts, "if I will not open the windows of heaven for you and pour you down an overflowing blessing." '

We are also told, 'You do not have because you do not ask' (Jas. 4:2). Do we not ask because we are frightened we are going to be let down? That betrays a lack of trust in our Father, who longs to display His blessings in us. Why not entrust Him with your family and friends today; with those problems and heartaches which you have carried so long?

'Come to me, all you who are weary and burdened, and I will give you rest. Take my yoke upon you and learn from me, for I am humble and gentle in heart, and you will find rest for your souls. For my yoke is easy and my burden is light.' (Mat. 11:28–30).

Alongside this story in Luke 11, I can place an incident from my own experience which God used to show me that exactly the same principles of prayer applies today as Jesus taught His disciples.

I was in my late teens and working in a bank in Lincoln, when one day the accountant called me into his office and asked if I would be prepared to go to London and do some relief work during the summer months, as they were very short staffed during that period. After some thought I agreed to do this and began to get excited at the prospect of new surroundings and new relationships. I was instructed I would be staying in a central London hotel along with about thirty or forty other bank clerks from around Britain; all there for the same purpose of helping out at different branches.

Although London was very much an unknown quantity to me, it was a challenge and I felt confident I would find my way around just fine. I explained the proposition to my parents and they agreed it was an opportunity not to miss.

I began to prepare myself for the great event and my mother laid down very clearly all the 'do's and 'don'ts' of the big city. That concerned me a little as I began to think seriously about the intended trip; but above and beyond that something else began to gnaw at me. Here was I, a young christian, going to live and share life for a period of time with 30 or 40 other girls, who as far as I knew would not be christians. How was I going to fare in that situation? Would I have the guts to witness to them? Would I have the courage to open my Bible and pray whilst sharing a room with non-christians? All these questions raced through my mind and I began to get panicky!

In desperation I started to pray, 'Lord put me in a room with a christian.' No sooner had I prayed that prayer, before a little voice from behind would mockingly say, 'What a stupid request. It will never happen. You're wasting your breath.'

Nevertheless, I persisted in praying the prayer numerous times each day, because as far as I was concerned, it was a matter of life or death that God heard and answered me. This regime continued until the day of my departure. Then taking a deep breath, I said goodbye to my folks still wondering why on earth I had agreed to undertake such an assignment. It would have been much easier to stay in Lincoln with the people I knew and loved and the security to which I had grown accustomed. But God had different plans. He had so much to teach me and to prepare me for what was ahead. Praise God He knows the end from the beginning and our

36

lives come under His Lordship. Although the way He takes us seems strange at the time, 'His plans are for good and not for evil, to give us a future and a hope' (Jer. 29:11).

I arrived at the hotel and was greeted by a young girl who had been appointed to make the bank girls welcome and show them to their rooms. She was rather loud and coarse and the conversation between reception and the fourth floor of the hotel was not very edifying. However, she unlocked the door of the room, flung it open and we walked in. I dropped my case, feeling totally exhausted and then came the bombshell; she announced that she would be sharing the room with me. My heart sank to my boots and so did my faith. I knew she was anything but a christian. I sat on the end of my bed feeling numb and with a hundred and one questions racing through my mind. What about prayer? And what about God who is supposed to answer prayer? Where is He? What is He doing to me?

I was about ready for picking up my case and catching the next train back to Lincoln, when I lifted my head and noticed there were three beds in the room. My spirit leapt as I thought 'Well Lord you have one more chance!'

Eventually, occupant number three arrived, Judy from Liverpool. My faith took another nose-dive as I looked at the poor girl. She was in a dreadful state. She sobbed and sobbed as she told me how much she hated London, the branch at which she was working and the hotel! Well this, I felt was really the end. I understood completely how the children of Israel felt when they accused Moses and the Lord of bringing them out of Egypt and into the desert to die. When I look back on the circumstances twenty-five years after the event, it's really quite laughable, but at the time it was very real. There was no way I was going to cope with these two girls. I felt utterly defeated. Maybe prayer worked for those Bible characters and special saints, which you read about in books, but it certainly didn't work for me.

I tried my best to pacify Judy, but nothing would console her. Then she began to tell me about a friend of hers called Ruth, who was in another room in the hotel. If she could share a room with her she would feel so much better. We went to see the powers that be, to ask if this was possible. This ensued in a great to-do. Names and room numbers were gathered in and re-shuffled and I eventually ended up sharing a room with Judy and her friend Ruth, who moved in complete with Bible. I was completely dumbfounded. God had cared for me so personally and individually that He had gone to all that trouble, both to protect my faith and show me that He was a mighty God that heard and answered prayer. Nothing was impossible for Him! 'My ways are higher than your ways and my thoughts than your thoughts' (Isa. 55:9).

I felt so ashamed at my lack of faith in the God I professed to know and love, that I climbed into bed, dived under the covers, asked for God's forgiveness and cried myself to sleep. That was just the beginning of a number of weeks of terrific fellowship and discovering more of this magnificent God that had brought about a miracle for one of the least of His children.

Towards the end of my time in London, Ruth and I had the joy of introducing Judy to Jesus and seeing her born again and brought into the family of God. What a privilege, God always gives us '. . . immeasurably more than all we ask or imagine' (Eph. 3:21).

If you put this story alongside the story Jesus told in Luke 11, you will see that you can extract exactly the same fundamental principles.

1) An intimate relationship.
2) A cry from the heart.
3) A measure of faith.
4) A determination to persevere.
5) Answers realised and God glorified.

When the cry comes from the heart, God takes notice and heaven goes into action. 'The eyes of the Lord are on the righteous and His ears are attentive to their cry' (Ps. 34:15).

God is looking for people whose praying is impassioned with His love and the same longing for His kingdom to come on earth, as it is in heaven. He's looking for people whose heart beats in the same way as His does.

'Arise, cry out in the night, as the watches of the night begin, pour out your heart like water in the presence of the Lord. Lift up your hands to Him for the lives of your children, who faint from hunger at the head of every street.' (Lamentations 2:19).

My praying had become very matter of fact and lifeless, just prior to my London experience. I had brought God down to my level and there was very little expectancy, if any. God used that incident and the fear that gripped my heart, to shake me out of my lethargy and to show me He was a mighty God, from whom I could expect great things.

How is your praying today? Have you come to a dry period, or run up a blind alley with no obvious way out? Have you got stuck in routine and tradition?

Turn to the Father today. He is as concerned about the condition of your heart, when you approach the throne of grace today as he was about the Israelites when he said

'These people come near to me with their mouth and honour me with their lips, but their hearts are far from me' (Isa. 29:13).

The Psalmist knew how important the heart was and what God required of Him as he came into His presence. He asked

'Create in me a pure heart, O God, and renew a steadfast spirit within me' (Ps. 51:10).

When we have found that cleansing and forgiveness from the Lord we can go on and ask the Father 'Restore to me the joy of your salvation and grant me a willing spirit to sustain me' (Ps. 51:12).

Take a look at the men and women of prayer in the

Scriptures and see how they poured their hearts out before God. The Father is not looking for some eloquent piece of expertise, but the longings and desires of your heart.

Remember the two men whom Jesus spoke about in Luke 18? They went up to the temple to pray. The Pharisee stood up first and prayed a great prayer. Everything was in order and beautifully pronounced. It must have been like music to the ears. And notice he was doing all the right things—fasting and tithing, but the Lord was not interested, because it was full of self and empty words.

However, the tax collector, the person that everyone tried to avoid, prayed a very different prayer. He understood his position before a holy God and then there was an outburst from his heart, 'God have mercy on me, a sinner.' The Scriptures tell us that this is the kind of prayer that's answered.

Again earlier on in Luke 18, Jesus uses the illustration of the widow and the unjust judge. The same principle is at the heart of the story, as we find in Luke 11. A plea that comes from our innermost being.

When we are young in the faith, babes in Christ, the Lord answers our cries fairly quickly, as in the story I shared about my time in London. I didn't need to wait too long for the answer. The Lord does that to encourage us in faith and trust. But as we grow older in the faith, so the Lord expects greater things of us. Sometimes there is a silence, or longer period of waiting, so that our faith in Him and His Word is tested and begins to grow strong. Job understood this when he said, 'But he knows the way that I take, when he has tested me I shall come forth as gold' (Job 23:10).

So don't be put off. Continue to cry out to God on behalf of those people and situations He has placed on your heart, but as yet do not seem resolved. God has His timing and your refining to consider.

It's a mystery that a mighty God should want our praying. But the fact is that He does. It is the anointed and appointed way that God has ordained to change circumstances and people's hearts to bring about victory. It is also the means by which we grow in fellowship and communion with Him.

'And will not God bring about justice for His chosen ones, who cry out to Him day and night? Will He keep putting them off? I tell you, He will see that they get justice and quickly.' (Luke 18:7–8).

On returning to Lincoln from London, filled with a new vision of what God can accomplish through prayer, I was totally unprepared for what I discovered in the fellowship. Some very sad facts had come to light that involved my closest friends; people who I loved and trusted and looked up to spiritually. I was devastated and didn't know where to turn. The people I would normally run to, I felt had enough on their plate. I churned the whole thing over and over in my mind, until I was almost dizzy and came to the conclusion that this one I needed to work out alone with the Father.

It was a desperately lonely time in my experience, but God will use the worst of circumstances and teach us invaluable lessons through them, if we will allow Him. How thankful I was for my London experience and of that new depth of relationship with the Father. I was certainly going to need it in the immediate days that lay ahead. All sorts of rumours would fly around and it was hard not to take any notice of them. In my loneliness I seemed to be a prime target for Satan. One day I would be standing on the promises of God's Word, the next day in the depths of despair. The big temptation was to throw caution and everything I believed to the four winds and join in the general morass that seemed to surround me, and almost engulf me at times. But I knew I couldn't deny the reality of God I had just encountered. I tottered on the brink of this indecision for weeks, until I realised that for my own peace of mind and in order to move forward, I needed to make a decision and stick by it.

Just before all this erupted I had been to see a stage production of the *Student Prince*. I loved the music from the show and used to play it often. One evening as I sat listening to this music, and feeling the weight of things, Mario Lanza began to sing 'I'll Walk with God'. The significance of the words hit me and I knew this was my moment of decision. I fell to my knees and made them my prayer.

'I'll walk with God from this day on,
His helping hand I'll lean upon
This is my prayer, my humble plea,
May the Lord be ever with me.

There is no death tho' eyes grow dim,
There is no fear when I am near to Him.
I'll lean on Him for ever
And He'll forsake me never
He will not fail me as long as my faith is strong,
What ever road I may walk along;

I'll walk with God, I'll take His hand.
I'll talk with God, He'll understand,
I'll pray to Him, each day to Him
And He'll hear the words that I say,
His hand will guide my throne and rod,
And I'll never walk alone while I walk with God.'

This was no light moment, but a serious watershed between me and the world. I had entered into a depth of commitment I didn't know I was capable of, and there was no turning back. I was on the Lord's side whatever the cost and wherever that path would lead.

Writing twenty-four years after that commitment, I can say with all honesty God has fulfilled every word of it and more. I am aware I have let Him down on many occasions but He has never let go of me, even though the path at times has been rough and steep. He has been a faithful friend in every aspect of my life.

You will now realise where the title of this book originates. When I was contemplating and considering the layout of the book and its contents, I took a brief scan of my life so far and its various milestones. Then the Lord showed me quite clearly that the commitment and decision I had taken that day was the point of no return. It was the day I decided 'I'll Walk with God'. I have been led down some strange and difficult paths since then, but never alone, and they have always, however long, led into God's glorious sunshine.

I realise, so much now, that God does not give us these experiences just for the sake of experience. They are for us to put what we have discovered into practice and to grow up in faith and fellowship with Himself.

'I am not ashamed, because I know whom I have believed, and am convinced that He is able to guard what I have entrusted to Him for that day' (2 Tim. 1:12).

Matthew 17:20

'If you have faith as small as a mustard seed, you can say to this mountain, "Move from here to there" and it will move. Nothing will be impossible for you.'

Bob Gordon

'Faith operates within human hearts. It is as we open ourselves inwardly to God that faith begins to work. The men or women who want to live by faith need to be ready to take within themselves all the challenge and cost of faith.'

Chapter 4

A Measure of Faith

Faith is a very important ingredient when we come to God in prayer. If this is an area where you feel a bit shaky, take heart; we all do from the greatest to the least of us. But God is willing to train us if we are willing to learn. Faith is not something you suddenly wake up with one morning and then 'hey presto' you've got it for the rest of your natural life. Faith is learned in the everyday situations of life that God presents to each one of us. There is no short-cut unfortunately. It's a tough lesson and an on-going lesson with which we need to wrestle, but also a rewarding one as we see ourselves grow and overcome obstacles in the power of Christ. We need to keep in mind the fact that this life here is a training ground. The Father is shaping us up to reign with Christ, that should help us understand the necessary 'square bashing' that God puts us through in order to equip us for that amazing task.

We must be like Christ who, 'Although He was a Son He learned obedience from what He suffered' (Heb. 5:8).

If we are real believers and serious disciples of the Lord Jesus Christ, then we know nothing that happens to us in our day to day living is by chance or coincidence. It has been planned or allowed by God to take us on or help us to grow in our faith and trust towards Him. This goes for bad, hard, tough and dark situations as well as the good; all are designed to make us mature in Christ. If you are asking the Lord for more faith, be careful! You can be sure He will place before you something that looks like a mountain. It comes, usually, in the form of a situation or a person. When we look within ourselves we know we haven't the answer. Then comes the invitation, 'Put me to the test.' This is how God beckons us on to greater steps of faith and trust in Him.

Watch as Jesus trains His disciples in faith. If you turn to John's Gospel, chapter 6 and the first fifteen verses, we read an account of how Jesus feeds the five thousand. Jesus and His disciples are up a mountainside and they see this vast crowd approaching. Jesus then turns to Philip and asks him, 'Where shall we buy bread for these people to eat?' And Philip answers, 'But we would need more than eight months wages for everyone to get a bite!' It didn't sound as if they would get very much to eat at that! It's very easy to sit down and analyse everything and try and work things out by reason and human thinking. But Philip must have known in his heart he hadn't got the answer and it was too big a question for him. How I praise God for verse 6 where it tells us that Jesus only asked Philip the question to test him, to see if he had an answer; because Jesus already had it in mind what He was going to do. That really gives me comfort and confidence. We come to the Lord with what we consider as massive problems and He tests us first.

Do we have an answer to meet the situation? As we ponder the question we very quickly realise we have no adequate solution to the circumstances. So when we have come to the end of our resources and begin to look to the Lord for our answers we can have every assurance that He knows the end from the beginning. For He already knows what He is going to do.

'Trust in the Lord with all your heart and lean not on your own understanding; in all your ways acknowledge Him, and He will make your paths straight' (Prov. 3:5–6).

Then Andrew pipes up. 'Don't suppose there is anything you could do with five *small* barley loaves and two *small* fish?' The emphasis seemed very much to be on the *small*. When we give our all to Jesus, however small we consider it to be, it is incredible how He can multiply things and give us back in amazing measure. This is one of God's promises,

> 'Give and it will be given to you. A good measure, pressed down, shaken together and running over, will be poured into your lap' (Luke 6:38).

The little lad who gave his lunch away probably thought, 'Well there goes my lunch. I'll just need to go hungry, or at the very most exist on a few crumbs.' Never in his wildest dreams did he expect to witness the biggest picnic he was ever likely to see; plus more than enough food for himself and everyone else to eat. We cannot outdo God. He is no man's debtor. He always does 'immeasurably more than all we ask or even imagine.'

Jim Elliott, one of the five martyred missionaries in Ecuador once penned some very searching words, 'He is no fool, who gives what he cannot keep, to gain what he cannot lose.'

Although the Lord has set before you a faith goal, which you with His divine help need to tackle, that is not the only thing He is working on. As you wrestle in prayer on behalf of others, keep your heart and mind open to what the Lord wants to say and do in your life also. This is the place where we are corrected, disciplined, encouraged, refined and changed from one degree of glory to another! Equipped for the Master's use. A great place of learning.

Having tested the disciples, Jesus then goes into action. The disciples eyes are fixed on His every move. First, He says to the disciples, 'Make the people sit down.' The Lord always works with great clarity and order and what He has to say is in very straight forward language. If the issue appears to be clouded and confused go back to the Lord for direction. But when you have heard a clear directive from Him, obey it. Then you can proceed with the next step.

Jesus then gives thanks for the loaves and fishes and begins to distribute them. The other gospels tell us the disciples helped in the distribution of the food. I am sure this was necessary as the crowd was enormous. You can imagine their feeling as Jesus placed a little piece of bread and a little piece of fish in each of their hands. If they looked at the small amount of bread and fish their hearts would sink and fear would grip them and if they turned and looked at the crowd, they would be overwhelmed by the vast number and the mammoth task they faced. But, if they kept their eyes on Jesus, they would see a miracle.

It's the same with us, we look at ourselves and our resources and we say, 'Who is sufficient for these things?' (2 Cor. 2:16, AV). Then we look at the odds stacked against us and they appear to be huge. But if we keep our eyes on the Lord and listen carefully for His strategy, then we will see God do mighty things, in ways that have never crossed our tiny finite minds.

'Is any thing too hard for the Lord?' (Gen. 18:14).

'God is not man that He should lie, nor a son of man that He should change His mind. Does He speak and then not act? Does He promise and then not fulfil?' (Num. 23:19).

I am going to share a true story from my own experience and show you how the Lord taught me faith as step by step I listened for His voice and His strategy. Remember all the Lord is asking for to begin with, is a 'mustard seed' of faith! It is very tiny, but in the end it produces a large tree.

On the Monday evening at the beginning of a week long mission, which Bob was leading, I was asked to speak to a young girl, who suffered from anorexia nervosa, whose marriage was on the rocks and the previous night had taken an overdose and tried to commit suicide. As I approached her, my heart sank. What had I to say to someone with such mountainous problems? I felt so inadequate in the human comprehension of them, let alone faith. I was defeated before I started. Faith, or at least the small amount I had, was fast disappearing.

When I eventually stood in front of the girl, she didn't

particularly want to speak to me. Everything I said was hopeless, pointless, useless and generally very negative. I talked around the usual trivia, as we do on such occasions, then she suddenly looked at her watch and said she needed to get home or her husband would beat her up! I began to panic on the inside but managed to say, 'I know you don't believe in prayer but I do.' The statement came out with such confidence, but inside of me it was a very different story of inadequacy and a question of how much I believed in the power of prayer. Could God really change and alter the circumstances of this young girl's life?

I asked her if I could pray for her before she went home, to which she replied, 'If you have to.' I quickly began to pray, going round in circles, making sure I included everything possible, quoting a scripture for good measure then she ran off.

I went back to where I was staying feeling utterly devastated and thinking this christianity is all very well for people with not too many problems, but what about a girl like this? Could the God I believe and trust in really come in power and give healing and victory over these huge problems? It was an incredible challenge to my faith. Then I got on my knees, placed the whole set of circumstances before the Lord, told Him how useless I felt and asked Him for direction and guidance as to how to tackle the situation. As it was such an involved situation and I didn't know where to begin, I began to pray in tongues.

When I had finished I listened for the Lord's voice. To my amazement He spoke, but it was in the form of a question. 'Search your heart and tell me what you can wholeheartedly believe I can do for this girl?' I really needed to be truthful. God knew my heart and it was no good trying to con Him. Sitting there I began to recall my conversation with the girl and I remembered her dark stony face. I was convinced nothing was penetrating or getting through to the hopelessness. I stripped myself bare before God and realised the most I could believe that God could do for her, was to put a smile on her face. I climbed into bed feeling very ashamed, but knowing I had been completely truthful with God.

The next night I saw the girl across the room. Her face didn't look so dark and I actually saw her smile once. At first I couldn't believe it, but then I began to praise God, as I realised He had been faithful and answered my prayer.

Then came the next question from the Lord. 'What do you think I can do for the girl now?' I knew that if God had to change the whole scene, then her husband needed to come into the picture. So I said 'OK Lord. I believe you could bring her husband along to one of the meetings.' So I began to pray to this effect. The Tuesday and Wednesday night went by, but there was no sign of her husband. Then on the Thursday evening she brushed past me in the pew and said, 'By the way this is my husband.' I was utterly amazed. I stood and gaped open-mouthed and recalled the faithfulness of God.

The message was pretty powerful that night and I could see that both of them were really convicted by what God was saying. Bob gave the opportunity at the end of the meeting for those who had been touched by God to stay behind for ministry. The rest could go through to the church hall for coffee. I was so excited. I thought, 'Lord you have really done it tonight.' However, then to my horror they just got up and walked through to the church hall for coffee. My heart sank at first, but then I quickly put my eyes back on the Lord and began to trust Him again. If He had brought them this far, then He was going to complete the job. How? I didn't know, that was His business.

Having ministered to a number of people I went through to have some coffee, only to find the couple still there looking at the bookstall. I went across and spoke to the husband and asked him how he felt about the meeting; to which he replied that it was very interesting, but he was an intellectual. I gave him a book to read and they both said they would be back.

I didn't see either of them to speak to until after the final Sunday morning service. As I was leaving, the girl pushed past me and said, 'Oh, by the way, can you remember that scripture you quoted the first night you prayed for me?' I was dumbfounded! I didn't think anything had got through that tough dark exterior yet God's Word had. It had penetrated right to her heart. What a lesson I had learned about the power of the Word of God! It certainly was 'living and active. Sharper than any double-edged sword, it penetrated even to dividing soul and spirit, joints and marrow, it judged the thoughts and attitudes of the heart.' (Heb. 4:12).

We began to talk and I pointed out to her that God had spoken in numerous ways through the week both to her and her husband. She admitted this was right and that she would like someone to pray for her as she committed her life to the Lord; and also to receive healing and know victory over her problems. I began to arrange for this to happen later on in the day, when her husband came back to see what the hold-up was all about. I explained to him what his wife was going to do and reminded him that I had sat next to him on Thursday evening and watched the tears course down his cheeks as God clearly spoke to him. He admitted that was true and asked if he could come along with his wife that evening for prayer and to recommit themselves to one another. By the end of that week God had done a complete work in that couple's life and marriage. I had learned so much more about faith and prayer and the Word of God that could reach even into the darkest heart.

I thank the Father for His infinite patience as step by step I stagger and grope towards all that He wants to perfect in my walk with Him.

I love the men and women of faith in the scriptures. They were flesh and blood just like us and the Bible doesn't hide the fact that they got it wrong from time to time. But they were people who loved their God and to whom the Lord entrusted some very difficult situations and directives in order to work out His purposes. We have so many lessons to learn from them.

Abraham was a man of faith. A man who knew his God and was obedient to God's calling. There was no hesitancy in

His heart when the Lord said, 'Leave your country, your people and your father's household and go to the land I will show you' (Gen. 12:1).

Abraham was obedient to the call. He didn't stop to argue or bargain with God, nor did he get Him to map out in detail where he was to go. His faith in God was such that he knew God's way was best and if he wanted to see progress and fruitfulness in his life, then he needed to pack his bags and follow where God was leading. So often we want everything in fine detail before we will move. The first six months laid out before us with all the securities we have grown accustomed to. That's not faith! Abraham's security was firmly fixed in God, not in his surroundings or even his family. We need to test what we believe to be a call of God, that is obviously necessary, but when we have established that the word comes from God, then we need to be prepared to move. This is faith, 'being sure of what we hope for and certain of what we do not see' (Heb. 11:1).

'By faith Abraham, when called to go to a place that he would later receive as his inheritance, obeyed and went, even though he did not know where he was going. By faith he made his home in the promised land like a stranger in a foreign country; he lived in tents, as did Isaac and Jacob, who were heirs with him of the same promise. For he was looking forward to the city with foundations, whose architect and builder is God' (Heb. 11:8–10).

Bob was just eighteen when God first spoke to him regarding the call on his life. During the first few years of our married life the whole question of 'full-time service' would arise. But just as quickly as it popped up it would be hastily buried again. It was a number of years later and in the middle of a very busy and successful business career, when we had the most to lose humanly speaking, that the call came afresh and this time needed a decision. Neither of us knew, as we stood up at the Keswick Convention in 1966 and dedicated our lives to the Lord and His service, where it would lead or what it would entail. We just knew God was speaking and we needed to respond. He needed to work out the details and we needed to learn daily how to trust Him. It wasn't an easy decision, but praise God He won! Little did we know then, that even over the first year, before Bob ever reached the college to begin his training, that decision was to be sorely tested. Each time we would examine the situation and go back to the Word the Lord had given us and to the commitment we made that day in Keswick. God was making sure we meant what we said. I thank Him for that. It taught us stickability, whatever the cost.

'No-one who puts his hand to the plough and looks back is fit for service in the kingdom of God' (Luke 9:62).

It is so much easier looking back over the last twenty years to see God's divine hand at work preparing our lives for such a day as this. We have had many ups and downs along the way, but we can both testify to the faithfulness of God through the years. We too can say 'Hitherto has the Lord helped us' (1 Sam. 7:12, AV) and testify that '. . . not one of all the good promises the Lord our God gave us has failed. Every promise has been fulfilled' (Josh. 23:14).

Sadly we have known friends, who have heard the call of God on their lives, but for one reason or another have ignored it, or walked away from it. To all intents and purposes, the reasons given usually appear pretty legitimate and for a time they are happy. However, deep down a sadness begins to creep in that nothing is able to quench, as they realise they have made a choice for the good instead of the best. Once we have tasted of God's rich grace and His ways of working, we are spoiled for anything else. Be careful with the decisions you make! Remember as disciples of Jesus we are building for eternity not just the here and now. However tough the road, however lonely, however uncertain the way ahead, our heavenly Father has His eye continually on us. His promise is 'I will never fail you, nor forsake you' (Heb. 13:5, RSV).

In chapter 15 of Genesis, verse 5, the Lord gives Abraham a promise. '"Look up at the heavens and count the stars—if indeed you can count them." Then He said to him, "So shall your offspring be."' The scripture then tells us, Abraham believed the Lord. But as the months and years began to pass by and neither Sarah nor Abraham were getting any younger, they decided to give God some assistance in fulfilling His Word. They hatched up a plan for Hagar to have a child by Abraham. This was not God's plan at all. God had a much superior plan to fulfil His promise to Abraham and to show him how great and mighty He was. When Abraham was one hundred and Sarah was very advanced in years, Isaac was born. 'Is anything too hard for the Lord?, (Gen. 18:14).

We can understand Abraham and Sarah trying to manipulate the situation, but they were wrong and it brought them a lot of trouble and not a little confusion. How easy it is for us to fall into the same trap. The Lord gives us a word of promise or lays a situation on our hearts and time marches on, but nothing seems to be happening. Don't give up! Bring it to the throne of grace. Lay it afresh before the Lord. Remember that's where it originated. Hold on to it and don't let go until you see it totally fulfilled in the way you know God meant it to be. Don't be satisfied with half-measure. Go for the real thing.

I well remember a few years ago, as we were standing in faith for the remaining money to come in for Roffey Place, and completion date was fast approaching. There was a suggestion we look at other properties and maybe buy one that was cheaper in price with the money the Lord had already provided. There was one such property on the market which we went to view. It was very tempting, but as we went back and looked again at Roffey, there was no doubt in our minds that the Lord had chosen that particular building and equipped it right down to the last teaspoon. We knew in our heart of hearts that looking at other properties was looking for an easy option. What we needed to do was to stand firm in faith that what the Lord had begun He would complete. How? We had no idea, that was His business. But we had His word, both directly from Him and from Scripture on which we could whole-heartedly rely.

Those of you who know the story of Roffey Place, or have read Bob's book, *Out of the Melting Pot*, will know how completely faithful God was to His word and His promise. There was no need for us to panic or try to manipulate the work of God, He was more than able to see this one through. Our eyes needed to be back on our all sufficient Father and trusting that word we had from the beginning. 'Ah Lord God thou has made the heavens and the earth by thy great power—nothing is to difficult for thee' (Jer. 32:17).

An incident from the life of George Muller, so ably illustrates the simplicity of faith in God. George Muller was on a ship approaching the shores of America. All around was shrouded in thick fog. Muller had an engagement to keep and was anxious that he was not late. He went to see the captain and to gain his verdict on how long they were likely to be held up by the weather. The captain was very unsure and the conversation proved inconclusive. 'I would like to help if I could,' he said 'but I am helpless.' Muller suggested they prayed. The captain obviously not convinced of the power of prayer got rather agitated and asked, 'Do you know how dense the fog is?' To which Muller replied, 'No my eye is not on the thickness of the fog, but on the living God who controls every circumstance of my life.' Needless to say as Muller finished praying and the captain returned to the bridge, the fog had lifted. That certainty and simplicity of faith in God is something I long for and hopefully work towards in my own prayer life. How well Muller knew his God.

Reach out to the Lord today. Ask Him to enlarge your heart and your faith for those people and situations for which you have been praying. Let us take our eyes off the fog and place them on a mighty God, who can break through the cloud and bring us into His wonderful sunshine.

Luke 11:8

'I tell you, though he will not get up and give him the bread because he is his friend, yet because of the man's boldness he will get up and give him as much as he needs.'

E.M. Bounds

'Persistence is the essence of true praying. Jesus taught that perseverance is the essential element of prayer.'

John Wesley

'Storm the throne of grace and perseverance therein and mercy will come down.'

Chapter 5

A Determination to Persevere

Persistence and perseverance are at the heart and very centre of prayer. The parable which Jesus told to teach his disciples to pray (Luke 11), very aptly illustrates how important perseverance is as a principle of true prayer.

Jesus was very careful to point out to the disciples that they must persist in prayer and not give up. The man in the story would not be put off even though everything seemed against him and the circumstances looked impossible. He didn't despair and nothing was going to quench his determination. His request was in earnest and came from a real desire to care properly for his friend. So, he would ask, seek and knock until he got an answer.

E.M. Bounds in his book *The Necessity of Prayer* says this:

'In the three words ask, seek, knock, in the order in which he places them, Jesus urges the necessity of importunity in prayer. Asking, seeking, knocking, are ascending rounds in the ladder of successful prayer. No principle is more definitely enforced by Christ than that prevailing prayer must have in it the quality which waits and perseveres, the courage that never surrenders, the patience which never grows tired, the resolution that never wavers.'

It's so easy to lose patience and throw in the sponge when the going gets tough and the Lord seems to be taking His time in answering our petitions. Jesus doesn't go into detail or explain why it is necessary to be so persistent in prayer, but from other scriptures we can see there is a purpose in what appears to be our human thinking and delaying tactics.

Firstly, the Lord has His timing. Secondly, He has our lives to fashion through the experience. Thirdly, it is to increase our faith. Fourthly, to teach us how to overcome Satan and his forces of evil.

Let's look at the Old Testament in 1 Samuel 1 and the story of Hannah. Here is a woman of persistence. Year after year Hannah would accompany her husband Elkanah and his other wife Peninnah to the temple and year after year she would make the same request of the Lord for a son. She just never gave up; she totally ignored all natural difficulties and temptations and pursued her consuming desire until the Lord answered. Now God would hear Hannah each time she prayed, but the answer was not immediate. Why? Well let's see if we can read between the lines of scripture and imagine what would be going on in Hannah's heart as she set out to plead with God for a son. We are told in verse 6 that Peninnah made fun of her and provoked her until she was so upset she began to weep and couldn't eat. I guess by the time she got to the temple Hannah's mind and heart would be in turmoil and she would begin to pray from very mixed motives. You can imagine there would be a fair amount of jealousy, resentment and bitterness swirling around inside her as she began to pray for that baby she so badly wanted. Notice she didn't make the state of her mind and heart an excuse for not praying. She knew the Lord had many things to sort out in her life as she communed with Him, but she also knew He was the only one who could meet her deepest needs.

Now look at verse 11 and see over the years the change that has taken place in Hannah's heart. Her whole attitude has altered. She set out by wanting something for herself, but she is now seeing things from God's perspective. This response could well have been what God was waiting for and working towards. You see Hannah didn't realise it, but after making her solemn covenant with the Lord, she had become a co-worker in God's divine remedy for Israel. A son was born to Hannah, but at the same time God had a man-child who would later become prophet and priest and restore a nation by faith. Not only do we learn from this story that it is necessary to prevail in prayer, but also that God has a plan and purpose for our lives and His timing is perfect. All Hannah wanted was a baby to cuddle and call her own but the Lord had much greater plans that would have far reaching repercussions for Israel as a nation.

In the New Testament in 2 Corinthians 12:1–12, Paul tells us about his 'thorn in the flesh.' Verse eight says, 'three times I pleaded with the Lord to take it away. You can imagine Paul's praying would be no half-hearted effort. Whatever the 'thorn in the flesh' was is immaterial, but it was such a wretched nuisance in Paul's life he wanted rid of it. The first thing the Lord reveals to him is why he has this 'thorn in the flesh', it was to keep him from conceit in his close walk with God. God told him He would not remove it, but promised 'My grace is sufficient for you, for my power is made perfect in weakness' (v9).

God has spoken. Paul had his answer and satisfied, he stopped praying and started to praise God. In verse 10 he can say quite honestly, 'For Christ's sake I delight in weaknesses, in insults, in hardships, in persecutions, in difficulties. For when I am weak then I am strong.'

In the light of God's promise of abundant grace, there is no way Paul is going to allow this area of weakness to take control. No way he is going to let it be an excuse for self-pity and despair. No. He's going to rise up and overcome it by the grace and power of Christ.

Our prayers are not always answered in the way we expect, but like Paul we pray on until we receive an answer, even if it is no; and then we act accordingly.

Wesley Duewel in his book, *Touch the World Through Prayer*, says:

'You have every right to be bold in your requests, to be persistent in prayer and to claim God's promises again

61

and again. Pray on until you get God's answer unless He guides you to discontinue your specific petition. He may do this by taking away your interest or desire, or by giving you an inner restraint that suggests this is not His will. However, until He does so press on in faith.'

Always keep open to God as you persist in prayer, so He can break and melt and mould you into the person He intends you to be. Maybe He has things to teach you, or maybe He has to discipline you in preparation for the answer, or maybe you have to be prepared, as in Hannah's case, to hand back to God the very blessing for which you have been praying. God will use every opportunity we give Him to build character and change us into His likeness.

In Luke 18 Jesus tells the parable of the persistent widow and the unjust judge. Verse 1 explains the purpose in relating the story; to show the disciples that they should always pray and not give up.

Every time I read this scripture I am challenged. How easy it is for our enthusiasm to diminish, especially as we see situations worsening instead of progressing, and the answer we look and long for seems a million miles away. But here Jesus encourages us to battle on, ignoring what appears to be the picture, humanly speaking, until we receive the answer.

This is what the widow was doing. She was determined to be heard and would not give up until she received justice. True praying is not for the fainthearted or the idle, but for those who are prepared to work. Praying in this dimension is exhausting because it involves our whole being, spirit, soul and body, but the outcome and reward is magnificent. God can work mightily and bring about His purposes through men or women who will give themselves wholeheartedly to prayer.

We see a tremendous persistence and faith on the part of the Canaanite woman in Matthew 15. The woman needed help urgently for her demon-possessed daughter and she knew Jesus had the answer. At first Jesus did not answer.

Then because she was so persistent and making such a nuisance of herself the disciples asked Jesus to send her away. Jesus turns to her and explains that He has been sent only to the lost sheep of Israel. But the woman still prevails upon Jesus for help. He turns again to her and says, 'It is not right to take the children's bread and toss it to their dogs.' Then comes that incredible reply, 'Yes Lord, but even the dogs eat the crumbs that fall from their master's table.' What perseverance and what faith!

There is a very strong link between perseverance and faith. At the end of the day, Jesus actually commends her for her faith, not her perseverance.

Look now at Luke 18 again and verse 8 where Jesus poses a very serious, but interesting question. 'However, when the Son of Man comes will He find faith on the earth?' Again faith is being linked with perseverance. The Lord tests us to see what confidence we have in Him. Do we really trust Him with the situations and people for whom we are interceding? Do we believe in the ability and willingness of God to answer our requests that we will persevere until we see victory? If Jesus was to return today would He find that persistence and faith in your heart? Are you prepared to do what Wesley suggests and 'storm the throne of grace and perseverance therein and mercy will come down?'

The Father wants us to be people, who not only trust in Him, but on whom He can rely. People whom He can entrust with different areas of the world. This is quite a responsibility. Therefore the Lord needs to teach us perseverance and reliability.

'Jesus said, "No-one who puts his hand to the plough and looks back is fit for service in the kingdom of God."' (Luke 9.62).

This began to happen to Bob and I fairly early on in our married life. After we returned from that week in Keswick, which was to change the course of our whole lives, we had some pretty tough decisions to face. In our naivety we thought we had done our bit for God by giving our lives to His service. Now we thought the doors, as we pushed them, would just fly open and it would be plain sailing. Not so! God had to test us as to how serious we were about that call.

Bob was working for an international pharmaceutical firm at the time and just prior to us going to Keswick had had interviews for a PR job in Head Office. We thought, now the Lord will be kind to us and when we get back home there will be a letter saying he hadn't got the job, so he could just continue in his work for another year then on into training. However, that was not to be. On our return there was a letter, but it said, '. . . pleased to inform you that you have been successful in your application . . . Come down to London and spend some time meeting your new secretary and seeing your new offices.' That threw us into some confusion and not a little panic! It meant nailing our colour to the mast a year before we intended to. (How wise God is!)

We now had a choice to make. Either explaining what had happened at Keswick and saying in the light of that Bob could not take the post. This of course meant taking the risk that they might say, 'Goodbye,' and then being out of work for twelve months. Or we could keep quiet about the events of the previous week and accept the post as if nothing had happened. What a dilemma! We wrestled and prayed about this one and in the end felt we must be honest and come clean whatever the cost or the consequences.

Amazingly, as Bob explained to those men of the world what had happened and how in all honesty he could not take up their offer, they listened. They said, 'Well we don't hope to understand you turning down a chance of a lifetime, but we do respect your decision.'

I want to thank God for that company, because right the way through Bob's four years in college and university they provided him with a job, a car and a rise in salary every summer vacation.

That was the first hurdle over. Again we sat back on our

laurels and thought that was it. But there was more testing to come.

Bob had successfully applied to the Northern Congregational College in Manchester to do a Certificate of Theology Course. He didn't have any A levels so he wasn't eligible to do a degree. He then had the task of applying for a grant but because the education department didn't recognise the Certificate of Theology Course his application was turned down. This was another blow. We sat and looked at each other and wondered if we hadn't made a terrible mistake. What was the Lord doing to us? If we were to pursue the path we had embarked on then it meant, after five years of marriage, Bob living in college and me going back to Lincoln to live with my parents. Surely, this was not what the Lord was asking. Even the friends we shared it with thought it was a tall order. It would be mad even to consider such a proposition.

Yet as we looked at that piece of paper which we signed at Keswick and heard again ringing in our ears the verse that had brought us to this crossroads,

'Anyone, then who knows the good he ought to do and doesn't do it, sins' (James 4:17).

We knew we had to go through with it; however much we didn't understand and however odd it looked. This was the way the Lord was taking us and we needed to trust Him.

It was a very hard year. We had no transport of our own, so the only means of communicating between the vacations was by letter or the odd telephone call when we could afford it. But God was at work, He knew what He was doing. Bob had no outside distractions—not even a wife—so he really ploughed on with his work. He took to Greek and Hebrew like a duck to water and the then Vice Principal, Edgar Jones, encouraged him to work towards taking his Mature Matric and apply for a university course. This he did and was successful. We were then given a grant, we found a suitable flat and I moved to Manchester.

God's plans for us were for good and not for evil, to give us a future and a hope. Although to begin with we were perplexed, the Father knew the end from the beginning and everything worked out far above anything we could ask or even imagine. It was a matter of obedience and loyalty to the Word of God and trust in the Father.

Faith that is not exercised or tested or put under pressure does not grow. It remains stagnant. But faith that is tried over a period of time is strengthened. Although it has been battered and buffeted from every angle it has stood the test of time.

'These (trials) have come so that your faith—of greater worth than gold, which perishes even though refined by fire—may be proved genuine and may result in praise, glory and honour when Jesus Christ is revealed' (1 Peter 1:7).

In the book, *Admiring God*, by Roger Steer, George Muller says,

'Ask and it shall be given you. There is a positive promise, but nothing as to the time. Seek and you shall find; knock and it shall be opened unto you. We have therefore patiently and quietly to continue waiting on God, till the blessing is granted. Someone may say, "Is it necessary I should bring a matter before God two, three, five or even twenty times; is it not enough I tell Him once?" We might as well say there is no need to tell Him once, for He knows beforehand what our need is. He wants us to prove that we have confidence in Him, that we take our place as creatures towards the Creator.'

Later on in the same book we are told that for thirty-six years Muller prayed every day for the conversion of two particular men. One was converted just before he died and the other soon after Muller's death. Praise God he never gave up, but he was faithful in prayer.

I often think of a land like China. Over the last few years

that country has begun to experience freedom and liberty, such as it has not known for many a long day. Stories of the christian church emerging and growing are thrilling to hear. Now this is not because latterly a few christians have decided to pray for China, but for decades men and women have not only been faithful in prayer, but some have laid down their lives for that country and are now in glory. We may die but true prayer never dies. The Lord works against a backcloth of eternity and weaves our prayers into His timing. Therefore, we need to live our lives and pray our prayers in the light of eternity and not just time. Remember God is moulding us to become like Jesus,

'. . . who for the joy set before Him endured the cross, scorning its shame and sat down at the right hand of the throne of God. Consider Him who endured such opposition from sinful men, so that you will not grow weary and lose heart' (Heb. 12:2–3).

It is five years ago now since the Lord gave me a word concerning Bob's life and ministry. Part of that word has been fulfilled, which has taken him through some pretty dark and hard times, but on into tremendous blessing. I could be satisfied with where we are now, but I know God has not finished yet. If I cease to pray now I know we shall miss the best. Therefore I intend to continue until I see the total fulfilment of all God promised. The christian life is not a bed of roses and the Lord may lead us down some dark and twisting paths, but He has terrific plans for us His children, if only we will reach for them.

'"No eye has ssen, no ear has heard, no mind has conceived what God has prepared for those who love Him" but God has revealed it to us by His Spirit' (1 Cor. 2:9–10).

Perseverance teaches us how to overcome the ploys of the enemy. Satan is such a wily being. He is a liar and delights to sow doubt wherever possible. All the more reason why we should know our God. We should know what He says in His written Word and what He has to say to us through His Holy Spirit today.

Job was a man of great patience. A man, the scriptures tell us, who was blameless and upright; one who feared God. Satan did His utmost to get Him to 'curse God and die.' First he attacked his possessions, then his family and after that his health. But through all his troubles and trials, and there were many, Job remained faithful and loyal to his God. As far as Job was concerned, God was sovereign. He was able to say 'The Lord gave and the Lord has taken away, may the name of the Lord be praised (Job 1:21). Then those amazing words in chapter 13 verse 15, 'Though He slay me, yet will I trust in Him.' (AV). And with great confidence 'I know that my Redeemer liveth' (19:25). What a man. He was so sure of his God and how to overcome the horrendous onslaught of Satan.

We are living this side of calvary and the resurrection. We have been given mighty weapons to come against Satan—the Word, the Blood and the Name of Jesus. Don't allow him to rob you of what God has already said and done in your life by his whispering lies. Come against him in prayer with the Word of God. He knows it is powerful and he recoils from it's truth. Don't allow him to threaten your inheritance in Christ, because you have the blood of Jesus to cleanse and protect you; and don't allow him to overwhelm you because 'Greater is He that is in you than he that is in the world.' Jesus is the name that stands above every name.

Learn how to persevere in prayer against Satan and see his kingdom overthrown and the kingdom of God and His Christ ushered in.

Matthew 6:6

'But when you pray, go into your room close the door and pray to your Father who is unseen. Then your Father, who sees what is done in secret will reward you.'

John Wesley

'Give me one hundred preachers who fear nothing but sin and desire nothing but God, and I care not a straw whether they be clergymen or laymen; such alone will shake the gates of hell and set up the kingdom of heaven on earth. God does nothing but in answer to prayer.'

Chapter 6

The Importance and Practice of Prayer

Not to pray is to sin

1 Samuel 12.23	'As for me far be it from me that I should sin against the Lord by failing to pray for you.' (NIV).
James 4.17	'Whoever knows what is right to do and fails to do it, for him it is sin.' (RSV).
Leonard Ravenhill	'We may call prayerlessness neglect or lack of spiritual appetite, or loss of vision. But that which matters is what God calls it. God calls it sin. Prayerlessness is disobedience, for God's command is that men ought always to pray and not faint. To be prayerless is to fail God, for he says "Ask of me."'
P. T. Forsyth	'The worst sin is prayerlessness. It is sin behind sin. And it ends in not being able to pray'.

The trouble with the scriptures and men of God like Ravenhill and Forsyth is that they don't beat about the bush and they are just a little bit too direct for us to handle. There doesn't seem to be a 'let out' clause!'

When God chose us in Christ He committed Himself to us and in turn we committed our lives to Him. But whereas God's promise to us is 'I will never leave you, I will never fail you' (Heb. 13:5), we treat the whole matter of prayer in a very nonchalant manner. If we've time, we pray, if we haven't, we don't. Our excuses are numerous; I know them well!

Meanwhile, the devil sits back, claps his hands and laughs, because by one way or another he has managed to hoodwink us into believing that there is no power in prayer, when all the time it is our most deadly weapon of warfare. It is, in fact, prayer that changes things, and not all our busy activity and discussion. I think we should write out clearly what Samuel Chadwick said and put it in a strategic place in our homes and churches, in order to remind ourselves of the necessity and importance of prayer over and above all else—'Satan dreads nothing but prayer . . . activities are multiplied that meditation may be ousted, and organisations are increased that prayer may have no chance. The one concern of the devil is to keep the saints from praying. He fears nothing from prayerless studies, prayerless work, prayerless religion. He laughs at our toil, mocks at our wisdom, but trembles when we pray'.

Prayer is the established and appointed way that God has devised for man to have fellowship with his Creator. Did you know that the Lord longs for your fellowship and companionship and He is grieved if you fail to meet with Him?

There is no substitute for prayer. Not all the sermons, talks, hymns, songs or even Bible reading can take the place of prayer. It is a daily necessity if we are to maintain a living relationship with the Lord. We ignore this fundamental truth at our peril and the end result is a severing of the very lifeline between us and the Father.

Prayer is also God's way of reaching the world, of touching men's lives with the gospel. Prayer is powerful, far more powerful than we appreciate. When you pray with a believing heart the whole of heaven goes into action. The angels are put on alert and stand ready to do the Lord's bidding. E.M. Bounds has a chapter in one of his books entitled, 'Prayer can do anything God can do'. So you see prayer is not only important to sustain our life in God, but also to be in partnership with Him in rescuing man out of his despair.

Prayer should be our way of life

1 Thessalonians 5.17 'Pray without ceasing.'

Luke 18.1   Jesus said, 'Men ought always to pray and not to faint.'

P.T. Forsyth   'Pray without a break between your prayer and your life. Pray so that there is a real continuity between your prayer and your whole actual life.'

It's not necessary for us to live in a convent or a monastery for prayer to be a way of life. No. This is for you and me with our jobs and homes and families. Granted it's not easy; but then there is always a price to pay for anything worth having. Doesn't our religion have a cross at the centre?

Those quotations from Paul and Jesus are not just quaint sayings that we can either take or leave. They are meant to be taken seriously. There is no need to water them down either, because you can be sure if God puts a command in His Word, then it's a real possibility. Earlier on in this book we noted that Jesus was in constant communion with the Father. But you may ask, how does one pray without ceasing? I can't be on my knees day and night. Of course not! You should set aside each day a time when you can meet with the Lord alone. At that time you can worship Him for who He is and thank Him for all that He has done on your behalf; bring to Him the deep needs of your life and your intercessions on behalf of others. At such times, God has a chance to speak to you. This is the place where He moulds and changes us 'from one degree of glory to another.'

However, the time arrives when we rise from our knees and go into the day. Nevertheless, our communion with God goes on, though at a different level. Forsyth, when speaking about the ceaselessness of prayer, says,

> 'It is the constant bent and drift of the soul . . . The note of prayer becomes the habit of the heart, the tone and tensions of its new nature, in such a way that when we are released from the grasp of our occupations the soul rebounds to its true bent.'

When the work we are doing, which requires all our attention, is at an end our hearts and minds should very naturally return to the Lord.

There are also jobs around the house and garden that don't demand our full concentration. This gives us a real opportunity to develop a relationship with the Holy Spirit, very much on a friendship basis. As we have already had time alone spent with the Father we have an entry into His presence, so that when people and situations come to mind that need our prayer we can lift them straight to the throne of grace. Prayer then becomes incessant and goes on at one level or another all the time. We begin to be conscious of God throughout the day and night too; because the Lord often wakes us in the night, or we have a dream and wake up with someone on our mind. That's the prompting of the Holy Spirit. Pray for that person.

This verse from one of Horatius Bonar's hymns sums up very adequately the ceaselessness of prayer:

> 'So shall no part of day or night,
> From sacredness be free,
> But all my life in every step
> Be fellowship with Thee.'

Prayer, as James Montgomery puts it 'is the Christian's vital breath, the Christian's native air,' and as Andrew Murray says 'is in very deed the pulse of the spiritual life'.

If we as human beings need to breathe twenty four hours a day in order to live, so it is exactly the same when it comes to our spiritual life—we need to breathe continually. Unfortunately, some of us have held our spiritual breath so long that we are going blue in the face, and there are some who are on the point of expiring. Come back to the throne of grace and find life.

Prayer should invade and pervade the whole of our life. God is not just vaguely interested in us, but He wants to be involved in every facet of our living. We are indeed His dwelling place.

The Practice of Prayer

'But when you pray, go into your room, close the door and pray to your Father, who is unseen. Then your Father, who sees what is done in secret, will reward you' (Matt. 6:6).

Make Time for God

1. I think we are all very aware that if we don't make time for God, there won't be any time. We can fill our days a hundred times over with all very necessary things. I am speaking to you as individuals now, not married couples or families. We will come to that later, but we all need time alone with the Lord.

a) *People who have a job of work or a profession they are involved in throughout the day, but no family.* You know what needs to be done before you go out in the morning and what needs to be done when you come home in the evening. But you say 'I'm so busy. You have no idea how much I have to cram into my day. And then there is the fellowship etc.' I do understand; but when we start making excuses, it's time to sit down and ask ourselves some questions. Am I a serious disciple of Jesus? If the answer is yes then you need to take a long, hard look at your day and see, either how it can be re-arranged or what needs to go to make room for prayer. Maybe it needs to start half an hour earlier! Remember the old saying that 'The person that is too busy to pray, is too busy!' I think a big lesson I had to learn, was when to say, *NO*. There are many demands made on our lives, good and legitimate demands, from our church maybe, but we know in our heart of hearts they are not right for us to take on board. You know the enemy is a past master at convincing us that the power is in the action. Remember he is a liar and a deceiver. If the action is not backed by prayer, it has no real effect as far as the kingdom of God is concerned. Where there's a will there's a way. It depends how determined you are.

b) *Mothers with tiny-tots.* I think this is the most difficult because your day is unpredictable. The times that were best for me were early morning feeds, when the rest of the house was still sleeping and the baby was feeding. Have something like the *Daily Light* near by or open the Psalms. Then just lift your heart to the Lord. Even if it is only five or ten minutes it keeps you in touch with the Father.

Another good time was when little ones have their rest in the middle of the day. I know the big temptation is to rush around and see how many jobs we can get done while they are asleep, but before you rush into the work, spend again five or ten minutes bringing those needs to Jesus. As your family grow up and are less demanding, so you can add to that five or ten minutes. If we have let things slip and made no effort during those early years, when little Tommy waves good-bye and goes to school, we realise that the time we were going to give to prayer has already been filled with some other necessity. If we maintain that foundational relationship with the Lord, then He can build on it.

c) *Couples.* It's good if you can get together, say two or three times a week and share what the Lord is saying and doing in your lives, both individually and as man and wife. It's encouraging to pray together for family, friends, church fellowship and the different situations that arise. I really appreciated the time we had in our church in Durham. In the morning, when everyone else had gone off in a variety of directions, Bob and I would sit down in the kitchen and we would pray for the people and situations where we needed to see God work. It was incredible. God broke through into the lives of those people whom we would term as hard nuts to crack, in amazing ways. Share scripture together too and encourage and build one another up.

d) *Families*. Again find a time that is going to fit in best with the family. Either straight after breakfast in the morning, if things are not too hectic in the mornings, or after supper in the evening. Don't make it an elongated affair. A verse of scripture or a Bible story and then a short time of prayer. Encourage the children to ask questions and join in the time of prayer. 'Train a child in the way he should go ans when he is old he will not turn from it' (Prov. 22:6).

Don't procrastinate any longer. *Make time for God.* It takes self discipline at first, but soon the discipline becomes not a duty but a joy.

2. Choose a time during the day or at night, when you are not going to be disturbed. Go into your room and shut the door. You will know best the time of day when you are alert. When the doorbell and telephone are unlikely to ring. Then do as the scripture says, find a room, go in and shut the door. Aim for as little distraction as possible.

3. Make sure you have plenty of time, not only to speak to God, but also to listen to His voice. If you are just a beginner, then I should start off by allowing yourself at least half an hour. By the time you read a passage of scripture, and meditate on it for five minutes, discern what the Lord is saying to you through it, then pray, you will discover half an hour just flies. As your prayer life and relationship with the Lord grow, expand the time. I got to the stage a little while ago, where I realised, I was trying to cram far too much into the first hour. I now use half an hour in the morning to read scripture and respond to what the Lord is saying to me through it. Then I praise God for who He is and what He has done for me and maybe worship the Lord with a song of praise. Later on in the day I find time to bring my needs and the needs of others to the throne of grace.

4. Keep a notebook and pen nearby to make a record of what the Lord is saying to you. It's good also from time to time to keep a prayer diary; with requests on one side and answers on the other. It's encouraging to look back over six months or a year and see how obedient you have been to the word God has spoken to you; what progress you have made and also how much has been accomplished through prayer.

5. *Be still* before God and don't rush into His presence (Ps. 46:10). He is our heavenly Father, but He is also the mighty God. Meditate on the Word; get acquainted with His voice. It's reported that Praying Hyde of India would approach the throne of God, with first a silence and then the words 'Oh, God!' Then he would repeat that until he knew he was in the presence of the almighty.

'Pray in the Spirit on all occasions with all kinds of prayer and requests. With this in mind, be alert and always keep on praying for all the saints' (Eph. 6:18).

6. Be specific. God needs to know what it is you are asking. It is no good praying for 'all the missionaries'—one would not know where to look for the answer. Also it is very important to be specific about sin in your own life; that needs to be confessed.

7. It is very helpful to pray aloud. This prevails your mind from wandering. I have found this very necessary. Most of us have many things swirling around in our minds and it is so easy to go off at a tangent. So I read the scriptures aloud, I praise God aloud and then I pray aloud. At first I was put off by the sound of my own voice, but I pressed on until the embarrassment disappeared.

8. Prayer lists are helpful. There will be people and situations for which you will want to pray, but when you have exhausted your lists, allow the Holy Spirit to lead you in prayer. He will bring to your mind things you have forgotten, or perhaps things as yet you know nothing of.

9. Don't go on feelings. Our spiritual life depends on obedience towards God and not on how we feel on any given day. There will be days when we are full of joy and can't wait to meet with God, and there will be other days when prayer is far from us and we want to run away from His presence. The Lord wants our fellowship and communion on both sorts of days. Be honest with Him. Tell Him exactly how you are feeling and why; but be open before Him. Allow Him to touch you, cleanse you and renew you in the power of His spirit. Pray on in obedience and in due course the feelings will return. P.T. Forsyth says

'Do not say "I cannot pray, I am not in the Spirit." Pray till you are in the Spirit . . . if you are averse to prayer, pray the more.' (He doesn't give an inch, does he?)

'Put me to the test says the Lord of hosts, if I will not open the windows of heaven for you and pour you down an overflowing blessing' (Malachi 3:10). (RSV).

10. Look for answers. If we observe what we have learned from scripture with its promises and conditions, and pray believing God will answer. Don't sit and try and work out how He is going to do it; that's His business. He is a God of variety and surprises and nine times out of ten the answer

comes from a very different direction from the one we are expecting.

11. Answered prayer builds faith and trust in God and results in thanksgiving and praise. You may start out with faith the size of a grain of mustard seed, but as God answers your prayers, so He expects your faith to grow. Look at the words of the Bible connected with prayer, 'all things', 'whatsoever', 'anything'. Romans 8:32 says

'He who did not spare His own Son but gave Him up for us all. How will He not also, along with Him, graciously give us all things?'

E.M. Bounds comment on this verse is,

'What a basis have we here for prayer and faith, illimitable, measureless in breadth, in depth and height! The promise to give us all things is backed up by the calling to our remembrance of the fact that God freely gave us His only begotten Son for our redemption. His giving His Son is the assurance and guarantee that He will freely give all things to him who believes and prays.'

12. For your encouragement, get hold of some biographies of the men of faith and prayer. See how God worked in their lives and remember He is the same God today and can work in exactly the same way. Look for instance at the work of E.M. Bounds, Andrew Murray, Hudson Taylor, Leonard Ravenhill, Campbell Morgan, George Muller, John Hyde, Charles Finney, John Wesley, William Wilberforce, Billy Graham, Colin Urquhart, Bob Gordon.

At the mere mention of the names of these magnificent saints of God, I begin to seriously wonder why I dare to write a book on prayer. I feel I have hardly begun and there is so much more to learn and ground to cover. But if I, through this book, can convince one more soul of the need for, and the power there is in believing prayer, then I shall be satisfied.

Remember that real believing prayer, generally speaking, is a lost and forgotten art. But it need not be so. Practise it daily and cultivate a relationship with the Holy Spirit, until it becomes your life.

Ephesians 3:20–21

'Now to Him who is able to do immeasurably more than all we ask or imagine, according to His power that is at work within us, to Him be glory in the church and in Christ Jesus throughout all generations, for ever and ever! Amen.'

Oswald Chambers

'There is no such thing as a private life—"a world within a world"—for a man or woman who is brought into fellowship with Jesus Christ's sufferings. God breaks up the private life of His saints and makes it a thoroughfare for the world on the one hand and for Himself on the other. No human being can stand that unless he is identified with Jesus Christ. We are not sanctified for ourselves, we are called into the fellowship of the Gospel and things happen which have nothing to do with us, God is getting us into fellowship with Himself. Let Him have His way, if you do not, instead of being of the slightest use to God in His Redemptive work in the world, you will be a hindrance and a clog.'

Chapter 7

Horizons Widened

In the first six chapters of this book we have been dealing with our personal communion and relationship with God which revolves around our own immediate circle and area of living. Now we need to extend our borders and widen our horizons as we are considering intercessory prayer, which takes us beyond the known and familiar into the very heart of God. We have seen God work in our own lives, our family, friends and fellowship, but He also calls us to be involved in His world.

Prayer, as you will have discovered, is a vast subject and covers every facet of our living; and because it is such a life-embracing subject it must be viewed against the large backcloth of the universe. You may well ask, 'What is the difference between prayer and intercessory prayer?' In brief, this is how I see it. Prayer, is us approaching God with our agendas. Intercessory prayer is God approaching us with His burdens, priorities and people. We need to make room for both in our lives.

An intercessor, is one who stands in place of another. God is always looking for intercessors. People who are prepared to be available to Him twenty-four hours a day and on whose hearts He can place His burdens. Also knowing they are people of determination, who will pray through until they receive the answer and see victory.

There is a real mystery as to why God needs our prayers and why it is that this is the force that breaks the power of evil and releases God's plans and purposes for the world; but I know that it is and that, it works. Andrew Murray, in

The Ministry of Intercession, lays a real challenge at our doorstep as individuals and as the Church of Jesus Christ. He writes:

'There is a world with its needs entirely dependent on and waiting to be helped by intercession; there is a God in heaven with His all-sufficient supply for all those needs waiting to be asked; there is a church with its wondrous calling and its surprises, waiting to be roused to a sense of its wondrous responsibility and power.

'There is a God of glory able to meet all these needs. We are told that He delights in mercy, that He waits to be gracious, that He longs to pour out His blessings; that the love that gave the Son to death is the measure of the love that each moment hovers over every human being. And yet He does not help. And there they perish, a million a month in China alone, and it is as if God doesn't move. If He does so love and long to bless, there must be some inscrutable reason for his holding back. What can it be? Scripture says, because of our unbelief. It is the faithlessness and consequent unfaithfulness of God's people. He has taken them up into partnership with Himself; He has honoured them, and bound Himself by making their prayers one of the standard measures of the working of His power. Lack of intercession is one of the chief causes of lack of blessing. Oh that we would turn eye and heart from everything else and fix them upon God who hears prayer, until the magnificence of His promises and His power and His purposes of love overwhelmed us.'

It is an indictment on those of us who call ourselves christians that such an accusation should be laid at our doorstep. When are we going to waken up to the fact that we are people of 'The Way', who have been called into partnership with God, to be co-workers, both in rescuing man out of his despair and turning Satan's cosmic system upside down? It is no good reading the newspaper and watching the news on television and then just lamenting over the state of the nation, when we can do something positively useful about it. So let us throw aside our depression and let us rise up and pray.

There was no one more surprised than me the morning I woke up with a terrific burden to pray for someone I only knew through reading the newspaper. I had seen God move in tremendous power in my own life, in that of my family and in our church fellowship. He had been teaching me so much about believing prayer, but this was something right outside my experience.

If you cast your mind back six or seven years, you may remember a family called Schild being kidnapped in Sardinia. A short time elapsed and Mr Schild was released in order to raise a ransom. Another period of time passed and Mrs Schild was set free. This left Annabel, their fifteen year-old daughter, alone with the kidnappers. I had followed the story in the newspaper and on television and thought what a dreadful crime against innocent people. Never had it once crossed my mind to pray for them; until that morning, it was a Wednesday morning, that I woke up with Annabel Schild weighing heavily on my heart.

This kind of thing had never happened to me before and I wasn't quite sure what to do with it. I felt in my spirit that the situation was serious, so I announced to the household that I would fast and pray during that day and try to discover what it was all about.

I hadn't a clue how to go about this venture, so I began to pray in tongues, asking the Lord to speak and direct my praying into the right channels. When I had finished praying in tongues, I gazed around the bedroom wondering, what next? Then my eyes landed on the *Daily Light* lying on my bed. The Spirit began to prompt again by saying the 3rd of February, the 3rd of February. I began to wonder if I was going round the bend or was this really from God. It was nowhere near the 3rd of February. The only way I could find out what was going on and what the Lord was trying to say to me was to turn up the 3rd of February in the *Daily Light* and see what it had to say. There to my amazement were, on the left hand page, many words of encouragement to me to 'Be strong—fear not—if God is for us, who can be against us? Thanks be to God, which giveth us the victory through our Lord Jesus Christ.' And on the right hand page were words that conveyed to me that the Lord had Annabel in His care and keeping.

'The darkness hideth not from thee. His eyes are upon the ways of man, and He seeth all his goings. There is no darkness, nor shadow of death, where the workers of iniquity may hide themselves. Can any hide himself in secret places that I shall not see him? Do not I fill heaven and earth? saith the Lord. Thou shalt not be afraid for the terror by night; ... nor for the pestilence that walketh in darkness ... Because thou hast made the Lord, which is my refuge, even the most High thy habitation; there shall no evil befall thee, neither shall any plague come nigh thy dwelling. He that keepeth thee will not slumber. The Lord is thy keeper: the Lord is thy shade upon thy right hand. The sun shall not smite thee by day nor the moon by night. The Lord shall preserve thee from all evil ... Yea though I walk through the valley of the shadow of death, I will fear no evil; for Thou art with me.'

Along with these words the Lord also gave me a picture of Annabel sitting in a very dark cave, but alive and well. I knew that I needed to pray against the evil her captors intended and pray for her release. From time to time throughout that day I went up to my bedroom and really began to enter a battle against the forces of evil. This was something new for me. God had given me a deep love for this young girl, whom I had never even met. I could identify with her in that dark cave, because the Lord had given me that picture and I now felt the battle was between life and death. I was determined Satan would not have the victory.

Towards the end of the afternoon I went along to pick up

my son Jonathan from school. He was to have a music lesson from my friend and prayer partner, Ann Thomas. I was handing him over into her care, when she said, 'A funny thing happened to me today. I got up with a real burden to pray for Annabel Schild.' I stared at her in amazement and we began to share all the events of the day. We both got so excited and felt very honoured and thrilled that God had chosen us, along with many others I am sure, to stand in the gap and be part of that mighty plan He had in mind for Annabel. We covenanted together to pray until Annabel was released, however long that might take.

However, Thursday went by and then Friday, with no word whatsoever about the Schild family on television or in the paper. Ann and I rang each other many times over those two days to see if either of us had heard anything. Then we would go over all the scriptures and the words the Lord had said to us. Had we got it wrong? Or did the Lord really speak to us? But each time we had to admit that what we had heard was real and we must continue, even if there was silence.

You can imagine our delight, when on the Saturday morning early news we heard that Annabel had been released and found wandering in the Sardinian mountains. We were elated and praised God for His mighty victory. As if that wasn't enough—the Lord is so gracious and always does far more abundantly above all we ask or even think; before the family left Sardinia some news reporters went out there to interview them and as you can imagine had a whole set of questions for them to answer. The last few questions were for Annabel and how she coped while she was on her own. The last question they asked her was, 'While you were alone in that cave, did you ever think to pray?' Her reply was, 'Funny you should ask that, but a few days before my release I prayed. I had heard of other people in my position who prayed and I thought I should try that and see if it works for me.' The reporter then asked, 'Do you think it had anything to do with your release?' Her reply was, 'I certainly do.' Then the reporter asked, 'Will you continue to pray?' and Annabel said, 'I will.'

From time to time I remember Annabel in my praying, that what the Lord began in her through that horrific experience, He will continue and complete.

After this experience I began to look at my newspaper and television through very different eyes. I needed to keep my heart and spirit open and sensitive to the Holy Spirit and to the people and situations He wanted to place before me. This was just a beginning and a preparation for all that lay ahead.

I was so excited having seen the Lord work in this miraculous way I wanted to know more of the working and ways of this mighty God. I took my concordance and the scriptures and began to search out the men and women of faith and prayer. I had read the stories many times before, but it had now hit me with a new force. These were real people with real situations who dared to believe God for the impossible. This was the same God, He hadn't changed. 'He is the same, yesterday, today, and forever' (Heb. 13:8).

I remember seeing an advertisement in one of the christian magazines for three of E.M. Bounds books on prayer. I had never heard of the man before and knew nothing of his writings but my eyes were glued to this advert and I knew I must get hold of these books. This I did and read them; chapter after chapter they were food for my soul. Having devoured those books, I went back again to the bookshop to see what else I could find. I looked along the shelves and my eyes stopped at a book called *Rees Howells, Intercessor*. Again I had not heard of the man, but knew this was the next book to read. How I was thrilled as I read this biography. You could almost see that man being changed from 'one degree of glory to another' as he was obedient to all the Lord asked of him. He was certainly taken through some strange experiences to test his confidence in God! I could hear the Lord say, 'This is the testimony of one man and the outcome of that walk of faith. This is what I am asking of you although the pathway and experiences will be different, the end result I am trusting will be the same.'

We were living in Harrow, during the time of these events and Bob was head of the Old Testament department at London Bible College, as well as maintaining his itinerant ministry around the country. But it wasn't long before the Lord altered all of that and brought us down to join Colin Urquhart and the Bethany Fellowship in West Sussex. This was a radical step and change in direction for us, but there was no doubt that it was of God.

I remember the day Bob came back from the Hyde, having met with Colin and men in similar ministries, (it was the 1st June, note) and said, 'Well, that's it. We are going down to Sussex to join Colin Urquhart and the Bethany Fellowship.' I stood there rooted to the spot in unbelief of what I was hearing. Bob had been down to the Hyde and met with those men on many occasions and had always come back, saying it was the last place to which he felt called! Now, I thought to myself, either this is a real word from the Lord or the man has had a brain-storm! I found myself asking the Lord to confirm that word to me that Bob had so clearly heard. I had been given a verse from the book of Haggai which I was mulling over in my thoughts, when I felt the Lord impress upon me to read the book of Haggai. I began to read the first verse and I am afraid I didn't get any further than the first few words, at least not for sometime! This is how it reads, 'In the second year of King Darius, on the *first day* of the *sixth month*, the word of the Lord came . . .' My eyes did the highland fling as I looked incredulously at the date and knew without a doubt that this was a word from God.

This new directive from God demanded we exercised faith and trust in Him in a greater way than we had before. We felt a bit like Abraham when the Lord said, 'Leave your country, your people and your Father's household and go to the land I will show you.' (Gen. 12:1). At least we knew the general direction in which the Lord was taking us, although we needed to see Him supply a house in the area and the finance with which to purchase it. I will never forget the look on the removal man's face as Bob, first picked the removal date and then asked him for a quote. When asked, 'What is your new address?' Bob replied by pointing on a map to the village of Handcross and said it would be in a five mile radius of that village. The man's face was a picture; but praise the Lord, whatever must have been swirling around in his mind at that moment, he booked the date, gave us a rough quote and took us on as serious customers.

God was so faithful to that step of faith and as Bob and I and our small household got down to serious praying and waiting on the Lord, He did indeed supply all our needs and more.

When we first moved down here the Lord provided us with the most lovely house and surroundings we have ever lived in. We marvelled at His generosity and felt we had arrived in paradise! However, the Lord did not allow us to 'rest in Zion' for too long, before He put, as far as we were concerned, a massive project of faith in front of us—Roffey Place. We soon learnt in the kingdom of God, change is here to stay! We also learnt that God had not brought us into this rich fellowship just for our own benefit. We were not a church, but a fellowship of people with a ministry of enabling the church and of revival for the nations.

I began to understand why the Lord had given me that experience of praying for Annabel Schild. I needed to know how to pray effectively for our nation and indeed His world.

Romans 8:34 Jesus

'Who is he that condemns? Christ Jesus who died—more than that, who was raised to life and is at the right hand of God and is also interceding for us.'

Exodus 32:31–32 Moses

'So Moses went back to the Lord and said, "Oh, what a great sin these people have committed! They have made themselves gods of gold. But now please forgive their sin—but if not, then blot me out of the book you have written."'

Romans 9:3 Paul

'For I wish that I myself were cursed and cut off from Christ for the sake of my brothers, those of my own race, the people of Israel.'

Homer W. Hodge

'We care not for your splendid abilities as a minister, or your national endowment as an orator before men. We are sure that the truth of the matter is this. No one will or can command success and become a real praying soul unless intense application is the price. I am even now convinced that the difference between the saints like Wesley, Fletcher, Edwards, Brainerd, Bramwell, Bounds and ourselves is energy, perseverance, invincible determination to succeed or die in the attempt. God help us.'

Chapter 8

Biblical Examples of Intercessors

This is the time when we get out the scriptures and enjoy and encourage our hearts as we look at some of the men and women of faith and prayer. It builds up our faith and spurs us on to greater exploits for God, as we watch God dealing with these saints of old, and bringing about His plan and purposes for His people.

In our consideration, we must first look at Jesus. He is the intercessor *par excellence*. He fulfils the work of an intercessor in every detail.

'Let us fix our eyes on Jesus, the author and perfecter of our faith, who for the joy set before Him endured the cross, scorning its shame, and sat down at the right hand of the throne of God. Consider Him who endured such opposition from sinful men, so that you will not grow weary and lose heart' (Heb. 12:2–3).

Obedience

Before the world was formed, there was God, Father, Son and Holy Spirit. Before the world was formed the great plan for the redemption of man had been conceived by the Godhead.

'Christ Jesus: Who, being in very nature God, did not consider equality with God something to be grasped, but made Himself nothing, taking the very nature of a servant, being made in human likeness. And being found in appearance as a man, He humbled Himself and became obedient to death—even death on a cross!' (Phil. 2:5b–8).

First of all we see Jesus, the Son, who is completely obedient to the Father and willing to take upon Himself and into Himself the whole plan of salvation; right through to Calvary and the victory of the resurrection morning. As we hear the call of God to intercession we have a choice of either ignoring it, or being willing to take up that call and take into ourselves the burden God is waiting to place in our hearts.

Praise God, Jesus was willing and faithful. There is a cost of time and priorities and the fact that it is done not in the glare of man, but in the private closet, alone with God. I am convinced that there will be many saints in glory, who are applauded by the Lord, for the hours they were prepared to spend before the throne of grace in battle, to make way for the gospel to run free in the hearts of men.

John Wesley said, 'God will do nothing, but in answer to prayer.' We need to recognise that God will not work without intercession.

'"I looked for a man among them who would build up the wall and stand before me in the gap on behalf of the land so that I would not have to destroy it, but I found none. So I will pour out my wrath on them and consume them with my fiery anger, bringing down on their own heads all they have done," declares the Sovereign Lord' (Ezek. 22:30–31).

What a tragic passage of scripture! What about God's call to you to stand in the gap? Are you willing?

Love

Love is the next essential characteristic of an intercessor.

'God so loved the world that He gave His one and only Son, that whoever believes in Him shall not perish, but have eternal life' (John 3:16).

We see Jesus' love for us demonstrated in so many different ways as we read the account of the Gospels, culminating in that amazing and horrific scene at Calvary. Such was His love for us. Jesus went all the way. Nothing and no-one was going to stand in His way or deter Him.

'Jesus took the Twelve aside and told them, "We are going up to Jerusalem, and everything that is written by the prophets about the Son of Man will be fulfilled and He will be turned over to the Gentiles. They will mock Him, insult Him, spit on Him, flog Him and kill Him"' (Luke 18:31–32).

Even knowing all this in great detail. Jesus never once wavered, but was willing to bear the cost of bringing men back into that covenant relationship with the Father.
'Greater love has no-one than this, that he lay down his life for his friends' (John 15:13) and that divine love that Jesus displayed is available to us as we enter into prayer on behalf of others, even people we do not know. We cannot be indifferent towards the people for whom we are praying. In the case of Annabel Schild, God gave me a love for her as if she was my own flesh and blood. 'Ask and you will receive.' The whole of heaven's resources are made available to the man or woman who will stand between God and man and intercede, according to the Spirit.

Insight

'For we do not have a high priest who is unable to sympathise with our weaknesses, but we have one who has been tempted in every way, just as we are—yet without sin' (Heb. 4:15).

This is Jesus who knows us through and through. He has a real grasp of the situation. He understood our plight and could see the mess we were in. He also knew the Father's plan and what it would take to recitify our predicament.

Again with Annabel Schild, the Lord gave me insight through those scriptures and that picture. He gave light and understanding where there was none. He gave me strategy and showed me how to pray. Don't grope in the dark when you can have the light of Christ. Ask God to give you a real understanding of the circumstances from His point of view.

Identification

'The Word became flesh and made His dwelling among us' (John 1:14).

The incarnation of Jesus goes way beyond our finite minds. That God the Son should set aside His glory for a time and come and take upon Himself flesh and blood. Live our life; know all of its ups and downs, its joys and sorrows, its many temptations; be truly man and yet know complete victory as He lived and worked in the power of the Spirit. We can join with the song-writer and say,

'O the love that drew salvations plan,
O the *grace* that brought it down to man.'

This is why we can approach the throne of grace with every confidence because 'A Man there sits at God's right hand, divine yet human still.' Jesus has lived our life, truly identified Himself with us and can empathise, not sympathise, in every situation. He intercedes for you continually.

Just in the same way as Jesus identified with us, so we need to identify with the people for whom we intercede. Know how to stand alongside them and how they feel as they are going through different trials and circumstances. The Lord, if we ask, will give us the ability to do this. I remember a cold shiver going down my back as I pictured Annabel sitting in that dark cave with many thoughts and fears racing through her mind.

Perseverance

Jesus never gave up on us! Even when confronted by Satan and offered the easy way out, Jesus would have none of it. He knew the Father's heart and plan so in His grace and strength He would march on; dealing with the Pharisees, the Sadducees, His own people who mainly rejected Him, and even His own disciples, who, at times, were so slow to understand. Still His goal was Calvary. We can just hear those haunting words from the Garden of Gethsemane,

> '"Father, if you are willing, take this cup from me; yet not my will, but yours be done." An angel from heaven appeared to Him and strengthened Him. And being in anguish, He prayed more earnestly and His sweat was like drops of blood falling to the ground' (Luke 22:42).

I shudder to think what would have been our end, if Jesus had deviated in any way from that plan of salvation.

When God has given you a burden, don't give up until everything that the Lord has laid on your heart has been accomplished. Sometimes we have short-term burdens that the Lord deals with very quickly and prayer is answered. But as your faith and confidence grow, so He trusts you with long-term burdens. These are the difficult ones, and Satan knows it. Don't be tempted to give up by his whispering doubts and deceptions. Consider Jesus! Be determined in your spirit to see it through, even if you don't live on this planet to see the final outcome, trust the Father, he specialises in victories!

Trust

The trust that Jesus had in the Father was implicit and explicit in all that He was and did. 'For I have come down

97

from heaven not to do my will but the will of Him who sent me' (John 6:38).

Jesus had a close relationship with the Father and because of this He knew that however hard and steep the road ahead, the Word and promise of the Father could be trusted, even though there was a cross at the end of it. Our minds and hearts can only glimpse that awful dark night when Jesus, who knew no sin, was made sin for us and God the Father had to turn His back on Him. The horror and agony and excruciating pain of the cross was bad enough, but to be cut off from the Father; I don't think we will ever be able to enter into or even marginally grasp the depth of loneliness and isolation that Jesus endured. But He trusted the Father that as He uttered those words 'It is finished,' the mighty battle was won; He had completed the work the Father had given Him to do. Now the Father would honour the Son. He would raise Him from the dead in glorious triumph.

'Therefore God exalted Him to the highest place and gave Him the name that is above every name, that at the name of Jesus every knee should bow, in heaven and on earth and under the earth and every tongue confess that Jesus Christ is Lord to the glory of God the Father' (Phil. 2:9–11).

Just as Jesus trusted the Father in every detail, so we need to trust Him. The words of promise and direction He has placed in our hearts, He will fulfil, if we persist and not break faith. When there are long silences or the situation appears to be deteriorating rather than improving, fix your eyes upon the Lord and your mind on His Word. Remember, 'The one who calls you is faithful and He will do it' (1 Thess. 5:24).

Moses

I love this man of God. He was an outstanding intercessor. I recall listening to stories in Sunday School about Moses and the children of Israel and thinking what a patient, long-suffering man he was. I am quite sure I would have got exasperated and given up on such a miserable, complaining bunch of people. But you see Moses had been called and commissioned by God from the burning bush and had a deep love for his people. What a different Moses we see at the burning bush compared with forty years previous to that experience; when, out of misguided loyalty and love for his people, he decided to take the law into his own hands, and do things his way. Unfortunately, it was not God's way. Moses had to flee from Egypt to Midian. The Lord was going to use this man in a powerful way, but he had many things to teach him first. Often during that long period Moses must have wondered what was the relevance of his desert experience, but the Lord knew what He was doing. He needed a man who was trained to hear His voice and His alone, who was humbled and disciplined in he ways of God; a man that God could trust, a strong leader for His chosen people.

Read through the book of Exodus and see how Moses kept in close touch with the Lord, and learned to listen for His strategy each step of the way. Firstly we see him before Pharaoh pleading on behalf of the Israelites, then at the Red Sea as the people begin to panic and wonder how God is going to rescue them out of this one. Had God brought them into the desert to die? Certainly not! (Exodus 14:13–16).

'Moses answered the people, "Do not be afraid. Stand firm and you will see the deliverance the Lord will bring you today. The Egyptians you see today you will never see again. The Lord will fight for you, you need only to be still."

Then the Lord said to Moses, "Why are you crying out to me? Tell the Israelites to move on. Raise your staff and stretch out your hand over the sea to divide the water so that the Israelites can go through the sea on dry ground."'

We know so well the outcome of this mighty act of God. As Moses was obedient to the Lord, so the Israelites walked through the Red Sea on dry ground, away from Egypt, Pharaoh and slavery, on towards the promised land.

Next we see Moses sweetening the waters of Marah so the people could drink; then the provision of the manna and the quail, food from heaven! Again in Exodus 17, as the people complain of being thirsty, Moses strikes the rock as instructed by God and out comes the water.

By this time, having seen so many mighty acts, you would have thought that those Israelites would be trusting God and their leader; but sadly as we turn to Exodus 32 and read the account of the golden calf we see the Israelites testing both God and Moses to the very limit.

Here in this episode we see Moses standing before God and His people as a mighty intercessor. Moses has been up Mount Sinai to receive the word of God for the people and as he descends he hears the noise of singing and dancing. He is so incensed at the scene he witnesses of the people dancing and worshipping the golden calf that he throws the tablets out of his hands, and they break in pieces. Not only is Moses incensed but God, Himself has had enough of this 'stiff-necked' people. In verse 10 of chapter 32, he says, 'Now leave me alone so that my anger may burn against them and that I may destroy them.' That was God's intention. But Moses leaves the people and climbs the mountain again to plead with God on their behalf. What a heart of love he has for his people, even after such devastating disappointment. In verse 31 and 32 you see him laying himself out before God for the Israelites, pleading 'Oh what a great sin these people have committed! They have made themselves god's of gold. But now, please forgive their sin—but if not, then blot me out of the book you have written.' This is the heart of a true intercessor, willing to lay down his life for the people he loves. Moses was successful in pleading with God to spare his people and so the Lord does not destroy them, but leads them on towards the promised land.

Elijah

This is one of the Lord's great prophets. We take up the story in 1 Kings 17, where Elijah is telling Ahab, 'As the Lord the God of Israel lives, whom I serve, there will be neither dew nor rain in the next few years except at my word.' This man must have known his God to make such a prediction. The Lord then directs him to turn eastward and hide in the Kerith Ravine and promises him water from the brook and the ravens to feed him. God is a mighty provider. His ways and means far exceed our finite minds.

When the brook dried up the Lord had arranged for a widow woman from Zarephath to take care of Elijah. Remember the jar of flour and the jug of oil—they never ran out. Also how when the widow's son became ill and died, Elijah came before God and cried to Him to restore his life and God granted his request.

Next we see him confronting the prophets of Baal. He challenged them to set up an altar and prepare a bull, put it on the wood, but not set fire to it. Then they had to call upon their god to set fire to the altar. This they did but with no success. They shouted and danced around the altar, for long enough, but there was no response. Elijah then began to taunt them. 'Surely he is a god! Perhaps he is deep in thought, or busy, or travelling. Maybe he is sleeping and must be awakened.' So they continued until the evening, but there wasn't a flicker.

Elijah calls the people and prepares a second altar in exactly the same way, except he digs a trench around his altar. Having cut the bull into pieces, he placed it on the wood, then orders four large jars of water to be poured over the offering and the wood, three times. Elijah then steps forward and calls upon the name of the Lord to send the fire, so that they will see and believe that the Lord, He is God.

God honours his servant Elijah by answering his cry and the prophets of Baal are slaughtered. Ahab is sent off by Elijah to eat and drink, but the man of God climbs to the top of Mount Carmel, because he hears the sound of heavy rain.

What faith this character demonstrates as he sends his servant to go look towards the sea, seven times. Six times he comes back and says there is nothing, but still Elijah persists, 'Go back.' The seventh time the servant reported, 'A cloud as small as a man's hand is rising from the sea.' That was enough for Elijah, the rain was coming; God was being faithful to His man Elijah.

James tells us in his epistle that Elijah was a man first like us. Today, as never before, we need men and women of faith, prayer and stickability who know their God and will keep looking out towards the sea, until they see all the promises of God fulfilled in our time.

Esther

Little did Esther realise the important role she would have to play in the deliverance of her people, when she was crowned queen in place of Vashti. Mordecai, the Jew, had brought Esther up and taken care of her like his own daughter, because she had neither father nor mother.

When the king was looking for another queen to replace Vashti, Mordecai had taken Esther along to the palace and put her in the care of Hegai, the king's eunuch. Esther was a very beautiful young girl and found favour with the king. Out of many possibilities, he set a royal crown on her head and made her queen.

Not long after these events, king Xerxes honoured a man called Haman. 'All the royal officials at the king's gate knelt down and paid honour to Haman, for the king had commanded this concerning him. But Mordecai would not kneel down and pay him honour' (Esth. 3:2). The scripture tells us that Haman was enraged when he discovered Mordecai would not bow down or honour him and because of this he cooks up a plot to destroy, not only Mordecai, but all of the Jewish people.

When Mordecai learns of this plot he is very distressed and sends word to Esther to go before the king and plead for mercy on behalf of her people. This was a very risky business, because no-one could approach the king in the inner court without being summoned. It could result in death, unless the king extended the gold sceptre. However, Mordecai pointed out to Esther that if Haman's plan went ahead, she as a Jew, even though she was of the king's household, would not escape. So Esther is encouraged by Mordecai to approach the king.

'And who knows but that you have come to royal position for such a time as this?' Esther was obviously a woman who knew her God and what to do in such a time of crisis. 'Then Esther sent this reply to Mordecai. "Go gather together all the Jews who are in Susa, and fast for me. Do not eat or drink for three days, night or day. I and my maids will fast as you do. When this is done, I will go to the king even though it is against the law. And if I perish, I perish"' (Esth. 5:15–16). Here was a woman who was willing to risk her own life in order that her own people might be spared.

You will know how the story continues, Esther dressed in her royal robes enters the throne room and approaches the king. As she does, so the king holds out the golden sceptre and she touches it.

The Lord had gone before this brave woman. He had heard her request and seen her fasting and had answered. The end result of this amazing story is that the very gallows that Haman built for Mordecai were used to hang Haman. Then 'Mordecai was made second in rank to King Xerxes, pre-eminent among the Jews and held in high esteem by his many fellow Jews, because he worked for the good of his people and spoke up for the welfare of all the Jews' (Esth. 10:3–4).

Esther was the right person in the right place at the right time. She was willing and open to God to be used, even at the risk of her own annihilation.

How would you fare if you were in Esther's position? And how much are we willing to be used in the place where we are? God is depending on us! Don't let Him down.

Daniel

Daniel was a magnificent man of prayer and discernment. We are told he was handsome, showing aptitude for every kind of learning, well informed, quick to understand and qualified to serve in the king's palace. Along with Daniel, being trained to serve in the royal household, were three other Israelites, Shadrach, Meshach and Abednego.

The scripture tells us, 'To these four young men God gave knowledge and understanding of all kinds of literature and learning. And Daniel could understand visions and dreams of all kinds' (Dan. 1:17).

They were invaluable to the king because 'In every matter of wisdom and understanding about which the king questioned them, he found them ten times better than all the magicians and enchanters in his whole kingdom' (Dan. 1:20).

Daniel was used on many occasions to interpret the king's dreams and he did this with amazing clarity. He held nothing back, good and bad news alike was given to these men. In chapter 5 of Daniel we read of the writing on the wall. In the middle of a great feast Daniel was called before the king to interpret this strange writing which appeared on the wall. Daniel feared no man, not even the king, and gave him the interpretation straight from the shoulder. 'Mene: God has numbered the days of your reign and brought it to an end. Tekel: You have been weighed on the scales and found wanting. Peres: Your kindgom is divided and given to the Medes and Persians (v26–28).

King Belshazzar can't have been overjoyed as he listened to Daniel's interpretation of the writing on the wall, but he obviously recognised the validity of it.

Verse 29 of chapter 5 says, 'Then at Belshazzar's command, Daniel was clothed in purple, a gold chain was placed around his neck, and he was proclaimed the third highest ruler in the kingdom.' The next verse verifies the truth of the interpretation. 'That very night Belshazzar, king of the Babylonians, was slain.'

After the death of Belshazzar, Darius took over as king. Darius noticed Daniel straight away; he was such an upright and outstanding man. This is what is said of him: 'Now Daniel so distinguished himself among the administrators and the satraps by his exceptional qualities that the king planned to set him over the whole kingdom' (Dan. 6:3).

It wasn't long before jealousy crept in among the other administrators and they set a trap for Daniel. A decree had been passed by the king that no-one should pray to any god or man during the next thirty days, except the king. Daniel knew exactly how to deal with this problem. He went home to his upstairs room, opened the windows towards Jerusalem and proceeded to pray to his God, three times a day. Of course, needless to say he was caught red handed and the punishment was that he would be thrown into the den of lions.

The king was very distressed when he realised the trap he had fallen into, because he had a very high regard for Daniel, but he was forced to adhere to the decree and pass sentence.

Daniel was subsequently thrown to the lions with his enemies rubbing their hands together and thinking that was the end of that little saga.

The king didn't sleep all night. He couldn't get Daniel out of his mind. So very early in the morning he rushed to the lions den and shouted for Daniel. He must have been stunned as Daniel answered back.

'"O king, live for ever! My God sent His angel, and shut the mouths of the lions. They have not hurt me, because I was found innocent in His sight. Nor have I done any wrong before you, O king."

The king was overjoyed and gave orders to lift Daniel out of the den. And when Daniel was lifted from the den, no wound was found on him, because he had trusted in his God' (Dan. 6:21–23).

What a testimony. We need men today who will stand firm and not deviate from the Word of God; men and women in all walks of life, from the high echelons of power down to the homes and streets where we live.

'Then King Darius wrote to all the peoples, nations and men of every language throughout the land:
"May you prosper greatly!
I issue a decree that in every part of my kingdom people must fear and reverence the God of Daniel. For He is the living God and He endures forever. His kingdom will not be destroyed, His dominion will never end. He rescues and He saves, He performs signs and wonders in the heavens and on earth. He has rescued Daniel from the power of the lions"' (Dan.6:25–27).

Wouldn't it be fantastic if such a decree was issued in our nation? It's up to us to live those lives that demonstrate the grace and power of the mighty God we serve.

'The people that do know their God shall be strong and do exploits' (Dan. 11:32, AV).

2 Corinthians 10:4

'The weapons we fight with are not the weapons of the world. On the contrary, they have divine powers to demolish strongholds.'

Ephesians 6:12

'For our struggle is not against flesh and blood, but against the rulers, against the authorities, against the powers of this dark world and against the spiritual forces of evil in the heavenly realms.'

E.M. Bounds

'Men born of prayer are the saviours of the state, and men saturated with prayer give life and impetus to the church. Under God they are saviours and helpers of both church and state. When the church is in the condition of prayer God's cause always flourishes and His kingdom on earth always triumphs. When the church fails to pray, God's cause decays and evil of every kind prevails. In other words God works through the prayers of His people, and when they fail Him at this point, decline and deadness ensue. Praying saints are God's agents for carrying on His saving and providential work on earth. If His agents fail Him, neglecting to pray then His work fails. Praying agents of the Most High are always forerunners of spiritual prosperity.'

Chapter 9

Prayer, Praise and Spiritual Warfare

Let me begin this chapter by quoting from S.D. Gordon's *Quiet Talks on Prayer*. In it he explains very vividly the over-all cosmic purpose of prayer. Every other aspect of praying fits in as we grasp hold of it from this perspective.

'Prayer has to do with conflict. The scene of the conflict is earth. The purpose of the conflict is to decide control of the earth and its inhabitants. The conflict runs back into the misty ages of the creation time.

The rightful prince of the earth is Jesus, the King's Son. There is a pretender prince, Satan, who is trying his best by dint of force to hold the realm and oust the rightful ruler. The rightful prince is seeking by utterly different means, namely by persuasion, to win the world back to its first allegiance. He had a fierce set-to with the pretender and after a series of victories won the great victory of the resurrection morning. There is one peculiarity of this conflict making it different from all others; namely a decided victory and the utter vanquishing of the leading general has not stopped the war. And the reason is remarkable—the Victor has a deep love-ambition to win, not merely against the enemy, but into men's hearts, by their free consent. And so, with marvellous love-borne wisdom and courage, the conflict is left open for man's sake.'

The christian life is one of warfare. When we pray we engage in battle. No soldier joins the army and goes to war without knowing the basic rules and some strategy. We are God's co-workers, God's outposts on this planet. God is depending on our co-operation in regaining territory on behalf of the Lord Jesus Christ.

Know Your Leader

A soldier must, first and foremost, build up a trust in his leader. Jesus is our Captain. The success or otherwise of the battles you engage in will depend largely on your knowledge and trust in Jesus. By knowledge, I don't mean an intellectual accumulation of facts, but a personal heart knowledge of Him and how He feels and works. We are back to that intimate relationship again that I spoke of earlier in this book. It is of vital importance, don't neglect it. Spend time in His presence. Get to know His voice and learn to distinguish it from other voices in the noise of battle.

Know Your Enemy

Every army has its intelligence men. Men whose job it is to find out as much as possible about the enemy's movements. Just in the same way we need to be aware of our enemy and acquaint ourselves with his tactics. Some of the names given to Satan well describe his role in today's world, the god of this age (2 Cor. 4:4); the ruler of the kingdom of the air (Eph. 2:2); the evil one (1 John 5:19); your enemy, the devil—a roaring lion (1 Peter 5:8) and a murderer, a liar and the father of lies (John 8:44).

There are many other references to Satan, which help to build up a picture of the enemy we are up against. Don't underestimate him, he is wily and a deceiver, but know that Jesus has won the battle and that victory is ours through Calvary and the resurrection. He is not almighty, omnipresent or omniscient, like the Holy Spirit, he is limited. Don't allow yourself to be intimidated by him; bind him in the strong name of Jesus with the authority that

Christ has given you. Satan turns a blind eye to Calvary and the resurrection; he likes to pretend it never happened and so holds onto every inch of territory he can, until in the name and authority of Jesus he is forced to surrender. Don't give him a foothold in your life. Remember you have the Blood of Jesus that cleanses you from sin; the Name of Jesus that is above every name and the Word of God from which he recoils. He is after all a fallen angel, doomed for eternal destruction.

Know the weapons at your disposal

God's weapons have always been very different from those of the world. (2 Cor. 10:4). If we look at some of the Old Testament men who won mighty battles for the Lord, and look at the weapons they used, they are almost laughable. But these men trusted their God, and knew how to listen for His voice and strategy.

David was one such person. He was just a young lad, but he had learnt from an early age of the God of Abraham, Isaac and Jacob. When he came up to the battlefield with some supplies for his brothers, he was surprised to find the Israelite army on one side of the valley, quaking in their boots and Goliath on the other side shouting abuse —threatening what he would do to them. David was fearless. He had once killed a lion and a bear as he explained to Saul, so 'this uncircumcised Philistine will be like one of them, because he has defied the armies of the living God.'

Saul agrees that David can go and fight Goliath, but he must protect himself with a coat of armour and a bronze helmet. David tries these on and feels totally out of place in them. Quickly he strips them off, chooses five small stones from the stream and puts them in the pouch of his shepherd's bag and with his sling in his hand he goes out to face Goliath. Goliath roars with laughter and mocks as the shepherd boy approaches him, but David stands tall in God and reminds him,

'You come against me with sword and spear and javelin, but I come against you in the name of the Lord Almighty, the God of the armies of Israel, whom you have defied.' David continues, 'Today . . . the whole world will know that there is a God in Israel. All those gathered here will know that it is not by sword or spear that the Lord saves, for the battle is the Lord's, and he will give all of you into our hands' (1 Sam. 17:45–47).

We know the outcome of the story so well. David slays the giant with a stone from his sling.

I once heard Satan described as the man with no power, but with plenty of noise. That's just what Goliath was like that day—plenty of noise and everyone was taken in by it, apart from David. A lot of noise can cause confusion and panic and that's just what the enemy is banking on, trying to throw us off course. Let's do as the scriptures suggest on these occasions and keep our eyes fixed on Jesus. Hold fast to the promise, 'You will keep in perfect peace him whose mind is steadfast, because he trusts in you. Trust in the Lord for ever, for the Lord, the Lord, is the rock eternal (Isaiah 26:3–4).

David slayed Goliath and won the battle, but it was a triumph for the God of Israel, and glory to His name.

Gideon was another man the Lord used, to win the battle against the Midianites. He had his army whittled down from 22,000 men to 300 men. Then they were given trumpets and empty jars and torches; strange weapons, but they were prescribed by God and they worked! It was such a ludicrous set up there was no way either Gideon or His army could take any credit for the victory won that day. No, it was glory to God.

It must have been quite unnerving for the people of Jericho to see Joshua and his men march around their city every day for a week, blowing their trumpets. Possibly after a few days they got used to the sight and thought 'Well, it seems to be keeping them happily and it looks a harmless enough occupation.' What a shock it must have been for them on the seventh day when Joshua and his men marched around the city blowing their trumpets as usual, when all of a sudden there was a shout and the walls of the city collapsed! I have been to Jericho and seen the thickness of those walls. That had to be a divine act!

These are stories that we read from time to time and get excited about, but that is as far as it goes. The truth is that just as God provided weapons for those men, so He provides them for us today to fight our battles against Satan. Our weapons, in the world's eyes, look ridiculous. If the truth be known, there are times when we question their validity.

In Ephesians chapter 6 the Lord provides us with a full coat of armour to protect us against the devil's schemes.

Truth

'Stand firm then with the belt of truth buckled round your waists.' Know your position in Jesus. We don't rely on feelings, we rely on the truth as declared in scripture. We are heirs of the Father and joint heirs with Christ. Do not listen to the lies and doubts of the enemy, confront him with the truth.

Righteousness

'The breastplate of righteousness.' We need to be morally upright people. We need to allow ourselves to live under God's microscope, so that as He highlights those weakspots and wrong habits, with the help of His Spirit we can tackle them; don't let them develop and so give Satan a stronghold.

Peace

'Your feet fitted with the readiness that comes from the gospel of peace.' The enemy would like to cause an uncontrolled storm in our lives, but if we have that peace that passes all understanding guarding our hearts and our minds, then all he can do is ruffle the surface; it soon dies down. Remember the disciples in the boat when the storm blows up and the waves look enormous Jesus lies asleep and it appears He is unaware of the situation. The disciples by now are in a real panic and think they are going to drown, so they wake Him and ask Him to do something. With great calmness Jesus gets up and rebukes the wind and the waves and the storm subsides. Then He asks the disciples, 'Where is your faith?. Did you honestly think I was going to let you drown? Jesus knows all about your circumstances, He has them in hand, they are not out of control, however stormy it may look. Just tell Satan your peace rests in the finished work of Christ and the victory of the resurrection. It is something we know God has done deep down within our spirits, not just a transient feeling of well-being.

Faith

'Take up the shield of faith with which you can extinguish all the flaming arrows of the evil one.'

'This is the victory that has overcome the world, even our faith' (1 John 5:4). Faith and trust in God are like a shield; when the enemy throws those fiery darts they bounce off it. It is impenetrable. Don't allow unbelief to creep in otherwise the devil will have a hey-day.

Salvation

'Take the helmet of salvation.' Know to whom you belong.

'How great is the love the Father has lavished on us that we should be called children of God! *And that is what we are!*' (1 John 3:1). So often Satan tries to attack us at the level of our sonship. Just let him know your redemption is real and it is eternal, so there is no way he can rock that firm foundation that is in Jesus.

114

The first few parts of the armour are meant to be put on, like clothes, to protect us, for our defence against the enemy. The Word of God, prayer, and I am going to add praise, are weapons which we use for attacking the enemy. They are weapons of offence.

The Word of God

'The sword of the Spirit, which is the Word of God.' This is for hand to hand fighting. Jesus uses it very effectively when he has that confrontation with Satan described in Luke 4. First he attacks Him at the physical level. Jesus has been fasting, so the devil says to Him, 'You are the Son of God, tell this stone to become bread.' Jesus answers him straight from scripture, 'Man does not live by bread alone.' Each time Satan comes to Jesus to tempt Him, Jesus answers from the Word of God.

Then he takes Him to a high place and shows Him all the kingdoms of the world, and promises Jesus they will be His if only He will worship him. This must have looked a much easier way than that of the cross. But Jesus will have none of it and says, 'Worship the Lord your God and serve Him only.'

Satan then attacks Jesus' sonship and he leads Him to Jerusalem and to the highest point of the temple. 'If you are the Son of God, throw yourself down from here.' How Satan loves to cast doubt into our hearts, but Jesus was ready again with His answer from scripture, 'Do not put the Lord your God to the test.' After this, Satan found he was getting nowhere fast, so he departed. If we stand on the Word of God and persist in it, Satan has to go.

The Word of God is powerful, is sharp, does penetrate and get through when all other words fail. Satan knows this, but we need to get hold of it and not be frightened to stand our ground until Satan gives way and Jesus is in control.

I remember, once, as I faced a speaking engagement I was feeling very fearful. Thinking of the people I was going to address and what I was going to say, I could feel myself slipping from faith into despondency; until I took hold of the verse 1 John 4:18. 'There is no fear in love, but perfect love drives out fear.' I began to repeat this verse over and over until the reality of it gripped my heart and penetrated from my mind through to my spirit. I could feel it take root and the fear evaporate as Satan loosened his grip and the power of the Word of God won the victory.

On another occasion Bob and I were having a day out together, when on the way back, Bob had a fit of coughing, which resulted in a very bad asthmatic attack. It was so bad we had to stop the car and call for an ambulance. By the time the ambulance arrived, Bob was gasping for breath and really struggling. It all seemed to happen out of the blue, for no apparent reason. I had seen Bob ill before with asthma, but this seemed such a vicious attack and I was very frightened. I battled in prayer as we waited for the ambulance, it seemed like an eternity, then the Lord gave me a verse from the Psalms that I took hold of and began to pray that into Bob—'I will not die but live and will proclaim what the Lord has done' (Psalm 118:17). I knew this was not God's time to take Bob, but that the enemy was trying to obliterate God's man, and I was determined he would not win.

As the ambulance arrived and Bob was lifted into it, I was still praying this scripture and continued to do just that all the way back to the hospital. I am sure the ambulance men thought they had a case for the psychiatric unit as well as for casualty. But I could feel the fierceness of the battle and I wasn't going to give up until I saw victory. I was so grateful to the doctors and nurses in the casualty department for the speed and efficiency with which they were able to regulate Bob's breathing. The Word of God was powerful and had done what it said it would do. '[The] word that goes out from my mouth: It will not return to me empty, but will accomplish what I desire and achieve the purpose for which I sent it' (Isaiah 55:11).

Prayer

Prayer is a mighty weapon for warfare. God has made Himself subject to prayer and placed Himself under the law of prayer. Wesley reminds us that 'God will do nothing, but in answer to prayer.' E.M. Bounds says,

'Prayer is putting God to work. It puts God's work in His hands and keeps it there. It looks to Him constantly and depends on Him implicitly to further His own cause. To no other energy is the promise of God committed as to that of prayer. Upon no other force are the purposes of God so dependent as this one of prayer.'

Even as I write these words the poignancy of them hits me afresh, I feel responsible before God. How much has the kingdom of God advanced today, because of my praying. If what I have discovered about prayer is true, that it is the divinely appointed means by which Satan's kingdom is defeated and the reign of Jesus brought in, then I need to think seriously about my priorities in life.

I think if we can re-educate and grasp hold of the fact of how powerful and necessary prayer is, we will do ourselves and mankind a favour. The devil has done a masterly job over the years by hood-winking us into some little cul-de-sac, and reducing prayer to look like some kind of optional extra for the believer; thereby robbing us of our most deadly weapon. What a twister and a liar he is!

I once heard a young minister describe prayer as our 'intercontinental ballistic missile.' I thought that was a brilliant description. We need to understand that when we pray our prayers don't wander around in space like some lost satellite, but God is waiting to take them and put them to work. The purpose of an intercontinental ballistic missile is to hit right into the heart of enemy territory, where the trouble is. And that is exactly what prayer does; it knows no distance, boundaries or barriers, God can effect miracles if we are prepared to pray.

I included praise in this list of weapons, because in recent years I have found it to be very valuable and effective, in breaking the power of Satan. The most outstanding account in scripture of praise winning a battle is to be found in 2 Chronicles 20. The story starts with the Moabites and the Ammonites coming to make war on Jehoshaphat. Jehoshaphat is alarmed, but knows exactly what to do. He calls a fast and gathers the people together to pray. As they begin to pray and ask for God's help in the matter, Jehoshaphat lifts the name of the Lord high, so their focus is not on the vast army, but how great God is. 'O Lord God of our fathers, are you not the God who is in heaven? You rule over all the kingdoms of the nations. Power and might are in your hand and no-one can withstand you.'

You can almost see faith rising as the people confirm how great God is. Jehoshaphat continues, 'For we have no power to face this vast army that is attacking us. We do not know what to do, but our eyes are upon you.' Just then Jahaziel has a word from the Lord concerning the situation, 'Do not be afraid or discouraged because of this vast army. For the battle is not yours but God's. You will not have to fight this battle. Take up your positions; stand firm and see the deliverance the Lord will give you, O Judah and Jerusalem. Do not be afraid; do not be discouraged. Go out to face them tomorrow, and the Lord will be with you.'

When we have heard from the Lord and He has given us direction we can walk on with every confidence in our hearts. Jehoshaphat prepared the people for battle. '"Listen to me Judah and people of Jerusalem! Have faith in the Lord your God and you will be upheld; have faith in His prophets and you will be successful." After consulting the people, Jehoshaphat appointed men to sing to the Lord and to praise him for the splendour of His holiness, as they went out at the head of the army saying: "Give thanks to the Lord, for His love endures for ever." As they began to sing and praise, the Lord set ambushes against the men of Ammon and Moab and Mount Seir who were invading Judah, and they were defeated.' It is just incredible how if we call on the Lord and are prepared to follow His directives and pick up the tools He has given us, mountains crumble before us.

A few years ago I was with Bob on a mission. After the first evening celebration we were both concerned with the resistance we sensed in the church. It was like speaking through porridge; the Word was not getting through. The next day I felt constrained to go into the church and walk around the pews, praising the Lord, singing songs and quoting psalms. It looked kind of stupid, but I felt it was what the Lord had said and so therefore necessary.

There was no way I could explain or analyse what happened during that time; all I know is that when Bob preached the next evening, the Word flowed, people were brought into the kingdom and the atmosphere was as different as chalk is from cheese.

Just about a year ago Bob took our college students and staff to visit a very similar college to ours in Germany. This was a terrific experience for all of us. Everyone of us came home challenged in one way or another. The challenge for me personally was how they prayed and in particular praised! We prided ourselves that we knew how to praise, but having visited the Glaubenscentrum, we felt we had hardly begun. In every meeting the praise would continue for long periods; sometimes in tongues, other times in English. I could sense that something very important was happening in the heavenly realms, but didn't know quite what. So I asked the Lord to show me. In reply to my request He gave me a picture. He said, 'Imagine a stone in your garden, well embedded; and you pull and you tug until you have unearthed it. What do you see?, I thought a minute and then I saw lots of creepy crawly creatures scuttling around, because they had been exposed to light. They were looking for another dark hole to crawl into. The Lord said that is exactly what happens in the heavenly realms when you lift my name high and praise me. Those spiritual forces go into complete confusion, they are immobilised. Satan himself is paralysed and unable to give any directives. Therefore I am free to work. Never underestimate the power of praise—it is not a mindless exercise, on the contrary, it enables the Lord to operate in freedom and power.

Know how to be disciplined

Obedience and discipline are not very popular words, but they are key words when it comes to the christian life and daily walk with the Lord. It is up to us how we divide our time up on any given day. We are responsible before God for what we allow our eyes to see, our ears to hear and where we allow our feet to walk. It needs to be edifying and pulling in the one direction, so encouraging our walk in the Spirit. A soldier's ear is trained to know and understand the directives of His commander. If you watch an army parade and listen to the sergeant major giving the drilling instructions, you can't understand a word he is saying. But the soldiers know, their ears are trained to it, and if they step out of line, they are immediately corrected. Our ears need to be trained to hear our commander's voice and act accordingly. In a war a soldier does not question the rights and wrongs of his commander's directives, but obeys instantly, otherwise if there is lack of discipline it will result in confusion and the battle will be lost. Every soldier or athlete in training is being groomed in how to win, not to lose or even come second, but to be first to the winning post. Everything he or she does or is involved in during that time is totally supportive to that one end and goal. So it is with us as christians; we need to get rid of the things in our lives that hinder us and take our eyes off the winning post, and bring into action those things that are going to sharpen our footsteps and win the race. Let's aim to be able to say with Paul,

'I have fought the good fight, I have finished the race, I have kept the faith. Now there is in store for me the crown of righteousness, which the Lord, the righteous

Judge, will award to me on that day—and not only to me, but also to all who have longed for His appearing' (2 Tim. 4:7–9).

Know the cost

No soldier ever joins the army completely starry eyed and not taking into consideration the fact, that he must be prepared, if necessary, to pay the ultimate price, his life, to preserve the freedom of his country.

The ministry of prayer and intercession, in particular, is not a glamorous one, it's a costly one. We must be prepared to be made a thoroughfare for the world; to be broken on account of others; to feel the hurt, the pain, the tragedy of men and the awfulness of sin. To pray efficiently and effectively we need to be able to appreciate at depth the needs and heartaches of mankind.

When Jesus was calling His disciples He always made it clear that there was a cost to discipleship. There were no easy terms or creeping in at the back door. It was all or nothing, there were no half measures. But once that man or woman gave themselves wholeheartedly to the Lord, then the whole of heaven and the Father's resources were available to them.

'Then Jesus said to His disciples, "If anyone would come after me, he must deny himself and take up his cross and follow me. For whoever wants to save his life will lose it, but whoever loses his life for me will find it"' (Matt. 16:24–25).

Isaiah 64:6–7

'I have posted watchmen on your walls, O Jerusalem; they will never be silent day or night. You who call on the Lord, give yourselves no rest and give Him no rest till He establishes Jerusalem and makes her the praise of the earth.'

2 Chronicles 7:14

'If my people who are called by my name will humble themselves and pray and seek my face and turn from their wicked ways, then will I hear from heaven and will forgive their sin and will heal their land.'

Leonard Ravenhill

'Could a mariner sit idle if he heard the drowning cry? Could a doctor sit in comfort and just let his patients die? Could a fireman sit idle, let men burn and give no hand? Can you sit at ease in Zion with the world around you DAMNED?'

Chapter 10

A Call to Revival Praying

'"We wish revival would come to us as it came in the Hebrides," said a pastor recently. But fellow servant, revival did not come to the Hebrides by wishing! The heavens were opened and the mighty power of the Lord shook those islands because, "frail children of dust . . . sanctified a fast and called a solemn assembly," and waited tear-stained, tired and travailing before the throne of the living God. That visitation came because, He who sought for a virgin in which to conceive His beloved Son found a people of virgin purity in those souls of burning vision and burdened passion. They had no double motive in their praying. No petitions were coloured with desire to save the face of a failing denomination. Their eye was single to God's glory. They were not jealous of another group who was outgrowing them, but jealous for the Lord of Hosts, whose glory was in the dust, the "wall of whose house was broken down, and whose gates were burned with fire."' Leonard Ravenhill.

When the Lord first began to stir my complacent heart regarding the state of the church and our nation it was to books and stories of past revivals I turned! I picked them off the shelves of libraries, bookshops and home and read avidly. I couldn't get enough of them. It gave me such an overwhelming desire to see God move afresh in our time in that kind of revival power, that I was determined to find out the secret and the key of such awakenings. Having scanned the pages of many records of revival they told the same story; there was no secret elixir, the answer was prayer, prayer and more prayer. Every revival, in whatever part of the world, great or small, was born in prayer. It slowly began to dawn on me the message the Lord was trying to get through to me. I could almost see the divine finger point at me and say 'Lack of real prayer is the reason for you being in the state you are, for the church being in the state it is and your nation being at an all time low. Arise, shake yourself out of your lethargy, your ease in Zion, and pray.'

I then turned to the scriptures and thumbed through from Genesis to Revelation only to have the Lord underline to me that God's Word is a record of prayer—of praying men and women and their achievements. If I wanted to see happen in my day and age, the kind of events I read about in the Bible, then there was no escape, I had to pray.

I once read an account of when D.L. Moody came to England in 1872. He was here not to preach, but to listen to others preach, whilst his new church was being built. However, he was persuaded on one occasion to preach in a certain London pulpit. After the morning service he was totally depressed and confessed he had never had such a hard time preaching in his life. Everything was dead. Then the awful thought crossed his mind, he had promised to preach again in the evening.

When D.L. Moody entered the pulpit again that night and faced the congregation, he was conscious of a new atmosphere. As he drew towards the end of his sermon he felt compelled to give an altar call. At once 500 people stood to their feet. Thinking there had been some mistake he asked the people to be seated. Then in order that there might be no possible misunderstanding he repeated the invitation, only making it in more definite and difficult terms. Again the same number rose. Still thinking that something must be wrong, for the second time he asked the people to be seated and then invited all who really meant business with God to go through to the vestry. 500 passed through to the vestry and that was the beginning of a revival in that church and neighbourhood.

What was the mystery that lay behind these strange happenings? It transpired that when Dwight Moody preached in the morning, there was a woman in that congregation, who had an invalid sister. When she returned home she told her that the preacher had been a Mr Moody from Chicago. On hearing this the invalid sister turned pale, 'What' she said, 'Mr Moody from Chicago! I read about him sometime ago in an American paper and I have been praying to God to send him to London and to our church. If I had known he was going to preach this morning I would have eaten no breakfast. I would have spent the whole time in prayer. Now sister, go out of the room, lock the door, send me no dinner; no matter who comes don't let them disturb me. I am going to spend the whole afternoon and evening in prayer.'

There was no mystery! It just took one believing woman, who so felt the urgency of the minute, that nothing else mattered other than the reviving Gospel of Christ be made real for that congregation. Her prayers were surely answered!

Ours will be too . . . 'If we do our part, God will do His. Around us is a world lost in sin, above us is a God willing and able to save, it is ours to build the bridge that links heaven and earth and prayer is the mighty instrument that does the work. And so the old cry comes to us with insistent voice, "Pray brethren, pray."' E.M. Bounds.

Almost ten years must have passed since I first made this discovery and I committed myself to pray for a spiritual awakening in this nation. I have seen enormous changes in my own life, family and circumstances, for which I praise God continually. Incredible things do happen through Holy Spirit filled men of God, but I do still wait and pray to see such a powerful movement from the Almighty in this nation, that it will leave me trembling in awe before a Holy God.

In the sixties, seventies and beginning of the eighties, the motto you could have written across the nation was, 'I'll do it my way' or 'I am god of my own destiny'. Over the last twenty years for all our advancement in science, education and intellectualism, a gross deterioration has taken place in our society. The crime rate has soared. We open our newspapers and read of one crime more horrific than another. We seem to be experts at mugging, rape and child abuse; with the result that all around us we have had permissiveness, divorce and breakdown in family life. Many a time I have wondered before the Lord, what is it going to take to bring this pleasure seeking, self-centred nation to its knees and beg for mercy.

Then suddenly the word Aids appears on our screens and in our newspapers and hangs like the sword of Damocles over our nation and every nation worldwide. Fear and panic grip the people as they run to and fro seeking a remedy.

There is no known cure. The days of saying to the Creator 'I'll do it my way,' have come to an abrupt end. So man wanders around like a lost sheep without a shepherd, not knowing which way to turn. It's time to seek the Lord and return to His ways. But how? Who is going to point the way?

Unfortunately, the church, as portrayed through the media has lost all credibility to the average man in the street. They have no answers. The trumpet they sound has such an indistinctive note, it is lost and useless.

But praise God, that's not the end of the story. Our nation needs to know there is a church, a blood bought remnant, of true believing people from all walks of life around these islands of ours, who care and have the answer to man's deepest need. There is an urgent need to pray as never before. Firstly, for the men in this country, full of the Holy Spirit and boldness, whom God has raised up. Secondly, for the openings and opportunities that are needed in order to convey this message to men and women who would not darken the door of a church building.

'Blow the trumpet in Zion, sound the alarm on my holy hill. Let all who live in the land tremble for the day of the Lord is coming. It is close at hand' (Joel 2:1).

God has set the stage for us. Let's rise to the occasion, rub the sleep from our eyes, pick up our weapons and fight.

General Booth had this to say,

> 'While women weep as they do now I'll fight; While little children go hungry as they do now I'll fight; While men go to prison in and out, in and out as they do now, I'll fight—I'll fight to the very end!'
> 'Oh that you would rend the heavens and come down' (Isaiah 64.1).

May God help us to have the same love and determination of spirit as we intercede on behalf of our people.

Let us pray!